but :

complacency
compromise
compliance
conformity
&
Christ

by Brian Bailie

But if not

First published 2022 by Broncle Publications
www.broncle.com
Copyright © 2022 by T Brian Bailie
All rights reserved

Quoted text from the King James Version of the Bible
Public domain.

Quoted text from The Passion Translation®
Copyright © 2017, 2018, 2020
Passion & Fire Ministries, Inc.
Used by permission. All rights reserved.

Quoted text from The Real Anthony Fauci
Copyright© 2021 by Robert F Kennedy Jr.
Skyhorse Publishing Inc® New York
Used by permission. All rights reserved.

Quoted text from 'When It's All Been Said And Done'
by Jim Cowan Copyright © 1999 Integrity Music®
All rights reserved.

ISBN: 9798799844233

Imprint: Independently published

Acknowledgement

The primary inspiration for this work is the word of God.

While preparing this manuscript I have been greatly encouraged by God-inspired writers, whom I gladly acknowledge here: James Aladiran, Brian Blount, Gregory Boyle, Eric Carpenter, JT Carson, Frances Chan, Shane Claibourne, Mark Clark, Jarron Cooper, John Mark Comer, Ray Comfort, Robby Dawkins, Rod Dreher, JL Fuller, EW Kenyon, Wayne Jacobsen, Timothy R Jennings, David Jeremiah, Robert F Kennedy Jr., Brother Lawrence, John MacArthur, Robin Mark, Putty Putman, Jeremy Riddle, Brian Simmons, Ed Silvoso, J Patterson Smith, AW Tozer, Amir Tsarfati, Frank Viola, Matt Walsh, Andrew Wommack.

These other writers have encouraged my deeper reading through God's word, and a greater appreciation for the condition of the world and the times we are now living in.

Do not read this book, or any other book about God's word, on its own.

The only true source of truth comes directly from God. God speaks to each one of us through his word, which is the Bible.

Therefore I strongly encourage you to follow up any quotes from God's word used in this book with study of your own, reading the quoted text in context, be it a paragraph, or a page, chapter, or an entire book of the Bible; and allow God to speak to you directly from his holy word.

Most of the quotations in this book are taken from the King James Version of the Bible. This is not because I dislike other translations, (I happen to have many other translations of the Bible). The reason for quoting from the King James Version is simple: Throughout history, more than any other, the King James Version remains the translation that has perhaps inspired the most powerful revivals, bringing millions to know Jesus and accept salvation through him.

Dedicated to the glory of my loving heavenly Father and to the truth of his Holy Word.

Contents

Introduction	2
Crafty Counsel	5
Speaking lies in hypocrisy	7
Such a time as this?	29
The powers that be	33
Awake, put on thy strength	41
Forgers of lies, physicians of no value	47
Neither cold nor hot	55
Forsake the foolish	63
But if not	73
Conspiracy theologist	81
Complacency	89
Superficial faith	101
Revive as the corn, grow as the vine	109
Bold as a lion	119
A form of godliness	127
Asa, and trust	133
Is God pro-choice?	139
A foot out of joint	145
Days of Noah	151
God forbid	157
Shame and fear	165
Here am I; send me	171

May the God of our Lord Jesus Christ, the Father of glory, give unto you the spirit of wisdom and revelation in the knowledge of him: the eyes of your understanding being enlightened: that ye may know what is the hope of his calling, and what the riches of the glory of his inheritance in the saints, and what is the exceeding greatness of his power to usward who believe, according to the working of his mighty power, which he wrought in Christ when he raised him from the dead and set him at his own right hand in the heavenly places

Introduction

Things have come to pass in this generation that correspond to the beginning of the last days that are prophesied throughout the breadth of the Bible.

The recent global pandemic appears to be an unprecedented social and economic upheaval, probably the most apocalyptic season in living memory; but in the scheme of things, it may prove to be but a shadow of the trials, terrors and tribulation that the world will soon suffer.

At such a time as this the wheat is being separated from the chaff: the naïve Christian is being separated from the well-read Christian; the committed Christian is being separated from the superficial Christian.

When Moses sent twelve spies to scout out the Promised Land (Numbers chapters 13 & 14), ten of those men returned with negative reports of strongholds and giants too powerful to confront.
Just two men, Joshua and Caleb, reported positively of this land flowing with milk and honey, boldly declaring that with God's help they shall easily overcome their opposition and inherit what God had promised them.

This global pandemic, and the mendacious manoeuvrings of governments who have erred to introduce totalitarian tactics to manipulate and control entire populations is just the beginning of things.

The next global disaster, (be it war, climate change, or an economic disaster), may be the catalyst that introduces the prophesied one-world government, (which is already widely mooted by powerful people and others with the influence and motivation to make it happen), which will create a great and terrible Babylon.

And then the trials will become terrors, and the terrors will become tribulation.

Now is not a time for weakness.

Now is a time for the confidence and boldness of Joshua and Caleb; to trust in God through these trials to come, which are ultimately part of his plan for the last days prior to the Judgement.

Now is not a time to live by lies.

Now is a time to trust, and to live by truth.

Even the Spirit of truth; whom the world cannot receive, because it seeth him not, neither knoweth him: but ye know him; for he dwelleth with you, and shall be in you.
John 14:17

For, lo, thine enemies
make a tumult:
and they that hate thee have
lifted up the head.

They have taken
crafty counsel against thy
people, and consulted against
thy hidden ones.

Psalm 83:2,3

Crafty counsel

There are manipulators with immense wealth and influence who are orchestrating a devious global agenda.

These manipulators are naively lauded for their status and altruism, earning themselves international prestige, power and influence.

Their sinister agenda is coerced by their strategically positioned pawns in key areas of high-level influence, including: politics, broadcast news, entertainment, internet and social media, pharmaceuticals, finance, and government.

These manipulators have already succeeded in fulfilling a series of masterful and elaborate opening moves of a long prophesied checkmate on the human race.

However, these manipulators are in turn being influenced by a much more potent deceiver. The father of lies is ultimately behind this global agenda; and the trials and troubles that we face now are just a foreshadow of the sorrows soon to follow.

If a ruler hearken to lies, all his servants are wicked.

Proverbs 29:12

Speaking lies in hypocrisy

Blessed is that man that maketh the Lord his trust and respecteth not the proud nor such as turn aside to lies. Psalm 40:4

Overwhelming science has proven that vaccinated and unvaccinated people are equally likely to spread COVID; a study in Israel in September 2021 demonstrated that natural immunity provides 27-times better protection against COVID than the Pfizer vaccine. This is just one of twenty-nine recent peer-reviewed studies that vouch for the superiority of natural immunity over vaccination.

[sources: Sivan Gazit, Roei Shlezinger, et al, "Comparing SARS-CoV-2 natural immunity to vaccine-induced immunity: reinfections versus breakthrough infections" medRxiv 2021.08.24.21262415; Brownstone Institute, "Natural Immunity and Covid-19: Twenty-Nine Scientific Studies to Share with Employers, Health Officials, and Politicians," Brownstone Institute (Oct. 10, 2021)]

Britain's top vaccinologist, Andrew Pollard, admitted that the Oxford University's government-funded and patriotically ballyhooed AstraZeneca vaccine had failed to achieve sterilizing immunity in monkeys; the inoculated macaques, even when asymptomatic, and continued to support high viral loads in their nasal pharynxes.
[source: Luke Andrews, 'It can prevent pneumonia': Oxford professor running coronavirus vaccine trial comes out in its defence after all of the monkeys given the treatment catch the disease, The Daily Mail, (May 22, 2020)]

Leading virologists, including Nobel Laureate Luc Montagnier, pointed out that a non-sterilizing vaccine could not arrest transmission and would therefore fail to stop the pandemic. Even worse, vaccinated individuals, he warned, would become asymptomatic carriers and "mutant factories" blasting out vaccine-resistant versions of the disease that were likely to lengthen and intensify rather than abbreviate the pandemic.
[source: Veronika Kyrylenko, Nobel Prize Winner Warns Vaccines Facilitate Development of Deadlier COVID Variants, Urges Public to Reject Jabs, The New American, (May 20, 2021).]

Boosters became a wonderfully lucrative strategy for neutralising variant threats: the development of an mRNA platform for vaccines that, in theory, would allow them to quickly produce new "boosters" to combat each new "escape variant." This scheme was Big Pharma's holy grail. Vaccines are one of the rare commercial products that multiply profits by failing. Each new booster doubles the revenues from the initial jab. Since the National Institute of Allergy and Infectious Diseases co-owned the mRNA patent, the agency stood to make billions from its coronavirus gambit by producing successive boosters for every new variant; the more, the better! The good news for Pharma was that all of humanity would be permanently dependent on biannual or even triannual booster shots. Dr. Peter McCullough warned that mass vaccination with a leaky vaccine during a pandemic "would put the world on a never-ending booster treadmill." That kind of talk had Pharma popping champagne corks. In October 2021, Pfizer announced that it was projecting an astonishing $26 Billion in annual revenues from its COVID boosters.

[sources: Zane Rizvi, "The NIH Vaccine," The Public Citizen (Jun. 25, 2020), and; Alex Newman, Dr Peter McCullough on Vaccine Death Rate, Raccoon Medicine, (May 29, 2021), and; Associated Press, "COVID-19 Vaccine Boosters Could Mean Billions for Drugmakers," USNews (Sept. 25, 2021)]

August 2021, the director of Israel's Public Health Services, Dr. Sharon Alroy-Preis, announced half of all COVID-19 infections were among the fully vaccinated. Signs of more serious disease among fully vaccinated are also emerging, she said, particularly in those over the age of 60.

[source: "Vaccine Effectiveness Drops Further in the Over-40s, To as Low as Minus 53%, New PHE Report Shows – And That's a Fact." Will Jones, The Daily Sceptic (September 24, 2021)]

An October 2021 study by scientists at Harvard's T.H. Chan School of Public Health compared vaccination rates for 68 nations and 2,947 counties across America as of September 21, and compared them to COVID-19 cases per one million people. Their report concludes that nations and counties with higher vaccination rates do not experience lower per capita Sars-CoV-2 cases.
[sources: "Population Wide Epidemiological Geography Demonstrates Vaccination Doesn't Correlate to Reduction in SARS-CoV-2 Infection." TrialSite News (October 3, 2021), and; S.V. Subramanian, A. Kumar, "Increases in COVID-19 are unrelated to levels of vaccination across 68 countries and 2947 counties in the United States," European Journal of Epidemiology (September 30, 2021)]

Between December 14, 2020 and October 1, 2021, American doctors and bereaved families have reported more than 16,000 deaths and a total of 778,685 injuries to the Vaccine Adverse Event Reporting System (VAERS) following COVID vaccination. The Europeans' surveillance sites tallied 40,000 deaths and 2.2 million adverse reactions.
[sources: Found 16,310 cases where Vaccine is COVID19 and Patient Died, NVIC (From Oct. 1, 2021 release of VAERS data), and; Found 778,685 cases where Vaccine is COVID19, NVIC (From Oct. 1, 2021 release of VAERS data)]

Vaccine Adverse Event Reporting System data show the huge spikes of 69.84% of deaths occurring during the two weeks after vaccination, 39.48% within 24 hours of the injections. According to The Center for Disease

Control's fatality data, a COVID vaccine is 98 times more likely to kill than a flu vaccine.
[sources: Med Alerts, Found 14,925 cases where Vaccine is COVID19 and Patient Died (September 10, 2021), and; COVID-19 Vaccinations 98 Times More Deadly Than Flu Vaccines (According to VAERS Reports), TrialSite News, (August 28, 2021)]

A recent peer-reviewed study in the high-gravitas Elsevier journal *Toxicology Reports* found that COVID-19 vaccines kill more people in each age group than they save. According to that study the "best-case scenario" is five times the number of deaths attributable to each vaccination versus those attributable to COVID-19 in the most vulnerable 65+ demographic.
[source: Ronald Kostoff, Why Are We Vaccinating Children Against COVID19? Toxicology Reports, Vol 8 2021, pages 1165-1684]

Vaccine Adverse Event Reporting System recorded nearly 800,000 injuries by the 9½ months between December 14, 2020 and October 2021, with 112,000 classified as "serious." Pfizer either did not report several severe injuries—short of death—or deceptively deemphasized their severity, during clinical trials, including neurological harm, thrombocytopenia, blood clots, strokes, embolisms, aneurysms, myocarditis, Bell's palsy, Guillain-Barré syndrome, multi-organ failure, amputation, blindness, paralysis, tinnitus, and menstrual harms. More than 30,000 women in the UK have complained of menstrual harms.
[sources: Victoria Male, "Menstrual changes after covid-19 vaccination" BMJ (2021), and; MedAlerts, "5,990

cases where Location is U.S., Territories, or Unknown and Vaccine is COVID19 and Symptom is Amenorrhoea or Dysmenorrhoea or Menopausal disorder or Menopausal symptoms or Menopause or Menopause delayed or Menstrual discomfort or Menstrual disorder or Menstruation delayed or Menstruation irregular," MedAlerts/VAERS, (Oct. 1, 2021)]

September 2021, a scientific journal, *JAMA Neurology*, reported a new series of cases of cerebral venous sinus thrombosis (CVST) linked to COVID-19 vaccines, confirming the severity of the reaction and the associated high mortality rate, and another journal confirmed the resumption of hepatitis C in a patient related to the jab.
[sources: Sue Hughes, "CVST After COVID-19 Vaccine: New Data Confirm High Mortality Rate," MEDSCAPE, (September 30, 2021), and; Ruud Lensen et al., Hepatitis C Virus Reactivation Following COVID-19 Vaccination— A Case Report. Int Med Case Rep J 2021; 14: 573–576]

According to the Vaccine Adverse Event Reporting System, there have been 7,537 cases of myocarditis and pericarditis reported following COVID vaccines, with 5,602 cases attributed to Pfizer. Some 476 of these reports occurred in children from 12 to 17 years old.
[sources: MedAlerts, "Found 7,537 cases where Vaccine is COVID19 and Symptom is Myocarditis or Myopericarditis or Pericarditis," MedAlert/VAERS, (Oct. 1, 2021), and; MedAlerts, "Found 5,602 cases where Vaccine is COVID19 and Manufacturer is PFIZER/BIONTECH and Symptom is Myocarditis or Pericarditis," MedAlert/VAERS, (Oct. 1, 2021), and; MedAlerts, "Found 476 cases where Age is 12-or-more-and-under-18 and Vaccine is COVID19 and Manufacturer is PFIZER/BIONTECH and Symptom is Myocarditis or Pericarditis"]

An October 2021 study in the peer-reviewed journal *BioRxiv* by Stanford and Emory University scientists suggests that antibody levels generated by the Pfizer-BioNTech vaccine can suffer a ten-fold decrease seven months after the second vaccination. The scientists warn that the precipitous drop in antibody levels will compromise the body's ability to defend itself against COVID-19 if the individual is exposed to COVID.
[source: Mehul Suthar et al., "Durability of immune responses to the BNT162b2 mRNA vaccine," BioRxiv preprint (October 2021)]

A government-funded study in October 2021 confirms the decline in vaccine effectiveness in England, finding that the reduction in transmission "declined over time since second vaccination, for Delta reaching similar levels to unvaccinated individuals by 12 weeks for [the AstraZeneca vaccine] and attenuating substantially for [the Pfizer vaccine]." In other words, within just three months, AstraZeneca did nothing to prevent transmission, and Pfizer was scarcely better.
[sources: Sara Y. Tartof, Ph.D. et al., "Effectiveness of mRNA BNT162b2 COVID-19 vaccine up to 6 months in a large integrated health system in the USA: a retrospective cohort study." The Lancet (October 04, 2021), and; Will Jones, New Lancet Study Confirms Plummeting Vaccine Effectiveness, The Daily Sceptic (October 7, 2021)]

A heavily powered study published by *The Lancet* involved 3,436,957 Kaiser Permanente Southern California customers, and compared

infections and COVID-19-related hospital admissions of fully vaccinated to unvaccinated people over the age of twelve for up to six months. The researchers found that vaccine effectiveness against infection plummeted from 88% during the first month after double vaccination to 47% after five months. The researchers found vaccine effectiveness against Delta infection was 93% during the first month after double vaccination but dropped to 53% after four months.
[source: Sara Y Tartof, et al, Effectiveness of mRNA BNT162b2 COVID-19 vaccine up to 6 months in a large integrated health system in the USA: a retrospective cohort study, (Oct 4, 2021)]

An October 2021 investigation by Israel's medical authorities of a COVID-19 outbreak in a highly vaccinated population of health workers at the Meir Medical Center in Sheba recorded 23.3% of patients and 10.3% of staff infected, despite a 96.2% vaccination rate among exposed individuals. Moreover, the researchers recorded multiple transmissions between two fully vaccinated individuals, both wearing surgical masks, and in one instance using full PPE, including N-95 mask, face shield, gown, and gloves.
[source: Pnina Shitrit, et al, Nosocomial outbreak caused by the SARS-CoV-2 Delta variant in a highly vaccinated population, Israel, July 2021 (Sep 30, 2021)]

Vaccine trials and approval are mathematically misleading. Pfizer used a measure called Relative Risk instead of the far more useful Absolute Risk. During the six-month trial two

people in the placebo group of 22,000 died, and one person in the similarly-sized vaccine group died with COVID. Any virologist (or any child) could tell you that the true reduction of risk of 1/22,000 is too insignificant to make the vaccine even a minor barrier against the spread of COVID. Despite the truth that the reduction in risk was less than 0.01%, Pfizer claimed that the vaccine was 100% effective – because 2 is 100% more than 1. And they got away with it! However, this 1-in-22,000 advantage of preventing a single COVID death comes at the cost of a fourfold increase (4/22,000) in excess fatal cardiac arrests and congestive heart failures in vaccinated people.
[sources: Stephen J. Thomas et al., Six Month Safety and Efficacy of the BNT162b2 mRNA COVID-19 Vaccine, medRxiv preprint (July 28, 2021); and, Ronald B. Brown, Outcome Reporting Bias in COVID-19 mRNA Vaccine Clinical Trials, Medicina, Medicina, (Feb. 26, 2021)]

According to official Pfizer vaccine trial results, the vaccinated group suffered four-times the number of lethal heart attacks as the unvaccinated group. In other words, there was no mortality benefit from the vaccines: for every life saved from COVID, there were four excess heart attack fatalities; twenty people died of 'all-cause mortality' among the 22,000 recipients in the Pfizer vaccine group, versus only fourteen in the similar-sized non-vaccinated placebo group. This means that there were 42.8% more deaths in the vaccine group than the placebo group; therefore, peo-

ple who take the vaccine are increasing their risk of dying by 42.8%
[source: Stephen J. Thomas et al., Six Month Safety and Efficacy of the BNT162b2 mRNA COVID-19 Vaccine, medRxiv preprint (July 28, 2021)]

Gibraltar boasted 100% vaccine coverage of its population of 34,000 citizens by July 2021. In December 2020, prior to the vaccine rollout, Gibraltar's health agency had experienced only 1,040 confirmed cases and five deaths with COVID. After the vaccination blitz the number of new infections increased fivefold to 5,314, and the number of deaths increased nineteen-fold. 84 elderly people died immediately after vaccination.
[source: Gérard Delépine, High Recorded Mortality in Countries Categorized as "Covid-19 Vaccine Champions". Increased Hospitalization, Freedom of Speech, (Oct 1, 2021).]

United Kingdom had inoculated over 70% of the population with one dose of the vaccine, and 59% with both doses by July 2021. Nevertheless, by mid-July there was a surge of 60,000 new cases per day. Leader of the Oxford Vaccine Group, Andrew Pollard, Britain's leading vaccinologist, acknowledged before parliament that collective immunity through vaccination is a myth.
[source: Holly Ellyatt, "Here's why herd immunity from Covid is 'mythical' with the delta variant," CNBC (Aug. 12, 2021)]

British data shows negative vaccine effectiveness of -53% for the over-40 age group. Reported infections are highest in the double-vaccinated. This means that people aged over 40 who are fully vaccinated experience a 53% higher reported infection rate than unvaccinated. Instead of preventing cases of COVID, the vaccine is enhancing transmission.
[source: "Vaccine Effectiveness Drops Further in the Over-40s, To as Low as Minus 53%, New PHE Report Shows – And That's a Fact." Will Jones, The Daily Sceptic (September 24, 2021).]

Over a seven-month period preceding October 2021, some 60% of the 2,542 English victims of COVID were double-vaccinated. There were more deaths per capita among the fully vaccinated than the unvaccinated. The UK Office for National Statistics report on mortality rates by COVID vaccination status shows that for age-adjusted mortality rate, the death rate by October 2021 was higher among the vaccinated than the unvaccinated.
[source: A comparison of age adjusted all-cause mortality rates in England between vaccinated and unvaccinated. Norman Fenton and Martin Neil, Probability and Risk (September 23, 2021); and , SARS-CoV-2 variants of concern and variants under investigation in England. Technical briefing 23, Public Health England (September 17, 2021).]

Child vaccination is unethical. As of September 2021, an estimated 600 children had already died from COVID vaccines. A recent

study in *The Lancet* shows that a healthy child has zero risk from COVID; yet some 86% of children suffered an adverse reaction to the Pfizer vaccine in clinical trials; and one-in-nine children suffered a serious reaction that left them unable to perform daily activities.
[source: Sunil S Bhopal, et al, Children and young people remain at low risk of COVID-19 mortality. (May 1, 2021).]

COVID vaccines have caused cardiac arrest, blindness, and paralysis in children. The British National Health Service reported that emergency calls for cardiac arrests are at an all-time high since government began offering teenagers the COVID vaccines. NHS statistics reveal that COVID vaccines do not protect children from hospitalisation or death associated with COVID because healthy children are not being hospitalised or dying with COVID. There is no evidence that the vaccines have prevented a single child's death.
[source: "Investigation: Deaths among Teenagers have increased by 47% in the UK since they started getting the Covid-19 Vaccine according to official ONS data." Will Jones, The Exposé (October 2, 2021).]

Teen deaths among 15-to-19-year olds have increased by 47% in the UK since they started receiving the COVID vaccines. Since the COVID vaccines almost certainly causes more teen deaths and injuries than COVID, vaccinating this age group is highly unethical, and

any physician who inoculates a healthy child is committing serious malpractice.
[source: "Investigation: Deaths among Teenagers have increased by 47% in the UK since they started getting the Covid-19 Vaccine according to official ONS data." Will Jones, The Exposé (October 2, 2021); and, Sunil S Bhopal et al., Children and young people remain at low risk of COVID-19 mortality, The Lancet, (May 2021).]

Unvaccinated people are being blamed for spreading COVID. Data across multiple sources and studies depict a very different reality: Fully vaccinated people who contract the infection have as high a viral load in their nasal passages as unvaccinated people; this means that vaccinated people are just as infectious as unvaccinated people. Vaccinated people carry 251-times the viral loads of Delta and other mutant variants than they did in the pre-vaccine era, which means that vaccinated people are spreading concentrated viral loads of vaccine-resistant mutants to vaccinated and unvaccinated people alike.
[sources: Nguyen Van Vinh Chau et al, Transmission of SARS-CoV-2 Delta Variant Among Vaccinated Healthcare Workers, Vietnam, preprints with The Lancet (Aug 10, 2021); and, Lindsey Tanner, Mike Stobbe and Philip Marcelo, "Study: Vaccinated people can carry as much virus as others," AP News (July 30, 2021)]

There is overwhelming scientific evidence that post-COVID inoculations are both unnecessary and dangerous.
[sources: Wen Shi Li, et al, Antibody-dependent enhancement and SARS-CoV-2 vaccines and therapies, Nature Microbiology, (Sep 9, 2020); Nouara Yahi et al,

Infection-enhancing anti-SARS-CoV-2 antibodies recognize both the original Wuhan/D614G strain and Delta variants. A potential risk for mass vaccination?, Journal of Infection, (Aug 9, 2021).]

Fifty-two separately conducted studies have revealed that wearing facemasks does not reduce viral infection rates, not even in institutional settings like hospitals and surgical theatres.
[sources: Children's Health Defence 2020-2021; Jeffrey D. Smith et al, Effectiveness of N95 respirators versus surgical masks in protecting health care workers from acute respiratory infection: a systematic review and meta-analysis, CMAJ. (May 17, 2016).]

Twenty-five additional studies concur that facemasks are harmful to public health, causing a multitude of conditions, including: respiratory and immune system illnesses; dermatological, dental, gastrointestinal, and psychological injuries.
[source: Jeffrey D. Smith et al, Effectiveness of N95 respirators versus surgical masks in protecting health care workers from acute respiratory infection: a systematic review and meta-analysis, CMAJ. (May 17, 2016).]

According to government data, 85% of people who contracted COVID reported wearing a facemask. According to the top medical advisor to the US government, the only real benefit of wearing a mask is, "making people feel a little better."
[sources: Alex Gutentag, "The War on Reality," Tablet (Jun. 28, 2021); Edmund DeMarche, Fauci's controver-

sial '60 Minutes' interview about mask-wearing was one year ago, FOX News, (Mar 8, 2021).]

There was no convincing difference in COVID infections and deaths between laissez-faire jurisdictions and those that enforced rigid lockdowns with masks.
[source: Centers for Disease Control and Prevention, Association of State-Issued Mask Mandates and Allowing On-Premises Restaurant Dining with County-Level COVID-19 Case and Death Growth Rates — United States, March 1–December 31, 2020, MMWR, (Mar 12, 2021).]

Life expectancy in developed countries decreased by 1.9 years during the lockdowns. But because COVID mortalities were mainly among the elderly (the average age of death from COVID in UK was 82.4 years) the virus cannot be blamed for the cause of this dramatic decline in life-expectancy.
[source: S H Woolf, et al, "Effect of the covid-19 pandemic in 2020 on life expectancy across populations in the USA and other high income countries: simulations of provisional mortality data," BMJ 2021;373:n1343 (June 24, 2021); and, Jemima Kelly, "Covid kills, but do we overestimate the risk?" Financial Times (Nov. 20, 2020)]

Globally, it is estimated that 300-million people fell into dire poverty, food insecurity, and starvation as a result of lockdowns.
[source: Alex Gutentag, "The War on Reality," TABLET MAGAZINE (June 28, 2021)]

Medical treatments that were deferred because of lockdowns for cancers, kidney failure, and diabetes has killed hundreds of thousands of people, and created an anticipated tsunami of cardiovascular disease and undiagnosed cancer.
[source: Megan Henney, "COVID's economic fallout could elevate US mortality rate for years, study shows," FOX BUSINESS (Jan. 5, 2021); and, Francesco Bianchi, Giada Bianchi, and Dongho Song, "The Long-term Impact Of The Covid-19 Unemployment Shock On Life Expectancy And Mortality Rates," National Bureau of Economic Research (Dec. 2020, rev. Sep. 2021)]

Among children in developed countries, lockdowns dramatically increased rates of child abuse, isolation, depression, suicide, addiction, alcoholism, obesity, mental illness. Lockdowns are responsible for debilitating developmental delays and severe educational deficits in young children. Infants born during lockdown were short by an average of 22 IQ points, as measured on the Baylor Scale.
[source: CDC, Emergency Department Visits for Suspected Suicide Attempts Among Persons Aged 12–25 Years Before and During the COVID-19 Pandemic—United States, January 2019–May 2021, (Jun. 18, 2021); and, Ohio State University, "A third of teens, young adults reported worsening mental health during pandemic," OSU Press Release (Jul 12, 2021)]

Due to lockdowns in 2020, US workers lost an estimated USD$3.7 trillion. Contrarywise, US Billionaires gained USD$3.9 trillion. Some 493 individuals became new billionaires at the same time as an additional 8 million Americans dropped below the poverty line.

[sources: Viral Inequity: Billionaires Gained $3.9tn, Workers Lost $3.7tn in 2020, TRT WORLD (Jan. 28, 2021); Chase Peterson-Withorn, Nearly 500 People Became Billionaires During The Pandemic Year, FORBES (Apr. 6, 2021); Heather Long, Nearly 8 million Americans have fallen into poverty since the summer, WASHINGTON POST (Dec. 16, 2020)]

Lockdown winners include: Larry Ellison of Oracle, whose personal wealth increased by USD$34 billion; Mark Zuckerberg of Facebook, whose personal wealth increased by USD$35 billion; Sergy Brin of Google, whose personal wealth increased by USD$41 billion; Jeff Bezos of Amazon, whose personal wealth increased by USD$86 billion; Bill Gates of Microsoft, whose personal wealth increased by USD$22 billion.

[sources: Chase Petersen-Withorn, How Much Money America's Billionaires Have Made During The Covid-19 Pandemic, FORBES (Apr. 30, 2021); Samuel Stebbins and Grant Suneson, Jeff Bezos, Elon Musk among US billionaires getting richer during coronavirus pandemic, USA TODAY, (Dec 1, 2020).]

Lockdowns were used to accelerate construction of the 5G network of satellites, antennae, biometric facial recognition, and track-and-trace infrastructure. This infrastructure allows government and intelligence partners to: mine and monetise personal information of entire populations; to suppress dissent, and compel obedience to arbitrary dictates. And to manage the uprising of the population when

they wake up to the fact that government has stolen democracy, civil rights, and a whole way of life.
[source: Sue Halpern, The Terrifying Potential of the 5G Network, THE NEW YORKER (Apr. 26, 2019)]

World Health Organisation condemned the use of lockdowns as a means to attempt control of COVID. They predicted at least a doubling of child malnutrition because children were not getting meals at schools where parents of poor families couldn't afford them; the consequence of using lockdowns is that it is making poor people poorer.
[source: Spectator TV, "WHO Special Envoy on COVID - Dr David Nabarro on Lockdowns (Oct. 8, 2020)," YouTube ...of Record, 00:09:39.]

Only 6% of COVID deaths occurred in entirely healthy individuals; the remaining 94% were already suffering from an average of 3.8 potentially fatal co-morbidities.
[source: Centers for Control and Prevention, Weekly Updates by Select Demographic and Geographic Characteristics, (Oct 6, 2021).]

Studies by the US Department of Health & Human Services indicate that the Vaccine Injury Surveillance System (VAERS) is understating vaccine injuries by over 99%. Government bodies refused to recommend autopsies on deaths reported to VAERS; this allowed the agency to repeatedly make audacious, fraudulent declarations that all the 16,000 reported deaths following vaccination by October 2021 were 'unrelated to the vaccines.' In essence: the regulatory agencies abolished vaccine deaths and injuries by official decree.

[source: Ross Lazarus et al, Medicare paid hospitals $39,000 per deaths from treating COVID-19, The Agency for Healthcare Research and Quality (AHRQ), (2010).]

Government health agencies offered no advice concerning the use of tobacco (smoking/vaping doubles the death rates from COVID); people were not advised to get plenty of sunlight to boost natural Vitamin D, (which has been proven to protect against COVID); no advice was offered concerning diet or exercise, (78% of people hospitalised with COVID were overweight or obese); there was no recommendation to avoid sugar and soft drinks, processed foods, and chemical residues, (all of which amplify inflammation, compromise the immune response, and disrupt the gut biome which governs the immune system).

[sources: Elizabeth Fernandez, "Smoking Nearly Doubles the Rate of COVID-19 Progression," UCSF (May 12, 2020); Becky McCall, "Vitamin D Deficiency in COVID-19 Quadrupled Death Rate," Medscape (Dec. 11, 2020); Berkeley Lovelace, Jr., "CDC study finds about 78% of people hospitalized for Covid were overweight or obese," CNBC (Mar. 8, 2021); Carolyn Crist, "Study: In U.S., Lockdowns Added 2 Pounds per Month," WebMD, (Mar. 23, 2021)]

Social media, search engines, and broadcast news media made vaccine injuries and deaths simply disappear! Facebook, Google, and the television networks purged doctors and scientists who reported pathological priming, and censored reports about waves of other vaccine injuries. Social media platforms censored doctors who reported vaccine failures, harms, and deaths; and patients who reported their own injuries had their accounts deleted from social media.
[source: Jerry Dunleavy, "Republicans press Facebook for documents on COVID-19 origins 'censorship' and Fauci emails," Yahoo News (Jun. 9, 2021)]

The man that wandereth out of the way of understanding shall remain in the congregation of the dead.
Proverbs 21:16

With thanks to Robert F Kennedy Jr. for contributing the facts in this chapter from his extensive research.

None calleth for justice,
nor any pleadeth for truth:
they trust in vanity,
and speak lies;
they conceive mischief,
and bring forth iniquity

Isaiah 59:4

And then shall many be
offended, and shall betray one
another, and shall hate
one another

Matthew 24:10

Such a time as this?

Now is but a pale shadow of the totalitarianism, trials and tribulation that will follow.

This know also, that in the last days perilous times shall come. 2 Timothy 3:1

Now that the wicked have demonstrated their control of the masses, there is little to stop them.

It is a proven scientific fact that facemasks do not protect people from COVID infection: for a healthy person to wear a facemask is to live a lie: Live not by lies, but by truth.

It is a proven scientific fact that lockdowns of healthy people do not arrest the spread of COVID, but have caused enormous harm to millions of people: to comply with lockdowns is to live a lie: Live not by lies, but by truth.

It is a proven scientific fact that the vaccines offer minimal practical defence against COVID infection, but have caused injury and death to hundreds and thousands of people: complying with mandatory COVID vaccinations is to live a lie: Live not by lies, but by truth.

These statements about facemasks, lockdowns, and vaccinations are proven facts: They are not conspiracy theories.

Is there justification for masks and lockdowns?

Yes, of course there is justification for wearing a facemask, and for isolating people. God's word is very clear and specific about this.

Leviticus chapter 13 describes the precautions that must be adhered to when a person is suffering the very infectious condition of leprosy.

Verse 45 states that an infectious person must put a covering over their mouth.

Verse 46 states that an infectious person must be isolated.

In fact all fifty-nine verses of Leviticus chapter 13 go into great detail about containing a highly infectious disease.

However, only the person presenting symptoms of the infectious disease must wear a facemask; only the person presenting symptoms of the infectious disease must self-isolate.

Where government restrictions clash with God's word, is that perfectly healthy people presenting no flu-like symptoms of COVID have been told that they must wear a facemask, and must adhere to lockdowns and social-distancing. These directives have been scientifically proven to be ineffective and harmful; and they are unbiblical.

I know of some objectors to government mandates who have acquired forged vaccine passports and forged test results to avoid complying with government directives for mask-wearing and vaccination.
But using forged passes is also living a lie: Live not by lies, but by truth.

Now that those in alliance with the wicked have succeeded in effecting mass control and the submission of people to live by lies, what should we anticipate next?

(I am not a student of end times prophecy; if you want to learn about the last days, open your Bible alongside the teachings of experts such as Dr David Jeremiah, or Amir Tsarfati.)

It may be nuclear war; or rising sea levels and climate change decimating food production; or a massive global economic crash,...

Or, it may be a global eruption of Acquired Immune Deficiency Syndrome (AIDS) that is directly caused by the COVID vaccines and boosters; such an outbreak of this deadly condition to over 70% of the population [and over 90% of healthcare workers] would be catastrophic.

And then, according to God's word, the people will make themselves dependant upon a great and mighty false hope.

It will be a New Dark Age.

For as a snare shall it come on all them that dwell on the face of the whole earth.

Watch ye therefore, and pray always, that ye may be accounted worthy to escape all these things that shall come to pass, and to stand before the Son of man.

Luke 21:35,36

The powers that be

A popular excuse by Christians who choose to comply with ungodly government mandates is found in Romans chapter 13.

> The powers that be are ordained of God. Whosoever therefore resisteth the power, resisteth the ordinance of God: and they that resist shall receive to themselves damnation.
> For rulers are not a terror to good works, but to the evil. Wilt thou then not be afraid of the power? Romans 13:1-3

Paul would have been hypocritical if he meant that we are to obey our government in all things, because Paul disobeyed and ignored laws that caused him to be punished, imprisoned, persecuted, and ultimately executed.

In fact the Bible is peppered with godly people disobeying the worldly powers that be:

Daniel disobeyed an order to cease praying. **He kneeled upon his knees three times a day, and prayed, and gave thanks before his God, as he did aforetime.** Daniel 6:10

Shadrach, Meshach, and Abednego disobeyed an order to bow down to an idol. **Be it known to thee, O king, that we will not serve thy gods, nor worship the golden image which thou hast set up.** Daniel 3:18

Midwives disobeyed the order to kill all male Hebrew babies, and then openly lied to Pharaoh. **But the midwives feared God, and did not as the king of Egypt commanded them, but saved the men children alive.** Exodus 1:17

Rahab disobeyed the order to give up the Hebrew spies, lying to the king so that they were protected. **And the woman took the two men, and hid them, and said thus, There came men unto me, but I wist not whence they were:** Joshua 2:4

The people refused to obey King Saul's command to execute Jonathan. **God forbid: as the LORD liveth, there shall not one hair of his head fall to the ground:** 1 Samuel 14:45

Obadiah hid God's prophets from Queen Jezebel. **Obadiah took an hundred prophets, and hid them by fifty in a cave, and fed them with bread and water.** 1 Kings 18:4

Peter and John refuse to obey the authorities that had commanded them to stop preaching. **We ought to obey God rather than men.** Acts 5:29

And in Revelation, John tells us that the people who become Christians at that time will disobey the Antichrist and his government. **And as many as would not worship the image of the beast should be killed.** Revelation 13:15

Bring the argument for compliance to the powers that be into the 20th century, and consider the Christians in Nazi Germany. Was it good for a Christian to follow the dictates of a government led by Adolf Hitler? In fact Hitler used Romans 13 for his own propaganda purposes. After the war, how many Germans used the excuse, "But I was just following orders" ?

A notable voice of resistance in Nazi Germany was Lutheran pastor Dietrich Bonhoeffer, who was persecuted and executed for speaking out against the evils of his government: *"Silence in the face of evil is itself evil: God will not hold us guiltless. Not to speak is to speak. Not to act is to act."*

Submitting to totalitarian dictates that are designed to control citizens by fear-driven propaganda in respect of facemasks and lockdowns and ungodly vaccines, is to submit to evil; it is to submit to disobedience to God.

Jesus told us to submit to persecution for what is of God; he did not tell us to submit to evil so that we might avoid persecution.

Blessed are they which are persecuted for righteousness sake: for theirs is the kingdom of heaven. Matthew 5:10

There are good laws, which Christians are obligated to submit to; and there are wicked laws, which Christians have an obligation to resist. The apostles whom Jesus personally chose and taught, all suffered persecution by the worldly powers that be:

Andrew was crucified in Patras;
Bartholomew was flayed to death with a whip in Armenia;
Luke was hanged in Greece;
James the just was thrown from the temple and beaten to death in Jerusalem;
James the greater was killed by beheading in Jerusalem;
John died in exile in Patmos;
Matthew was killed by sword in Ethiopia;
Matthias was stoned and beheaded in Jerusalem;
Mark was dragged to death behind a horse in Alexandria;
Paul was beheaded in Rome;
Peter was crucified upside-down in Rome;
Philip was crucified in Phrygia;
Thomas was speared to death in India.

There is an undeniable pattern of persecution towards the apostles. Do you think that if they had submitted to the powers that be, kept their heads down and complied with the worldly authorities, things may have turned out a little easier for them?

Submitting to the powers that be is wrong when what they command you to comply with conflicts with God's word.

Many people like to think of following Jesus as a journey, or a lifestyle; but this isn't what we are taught in God's word.
We are taught to fight the good fight; put on the whole armour of God; to fight the battle well; and, to demolish demonic strongholds.

Too many Christians just breeze through life, not taking their salvation seriously; they consider salvation only as a blessing, and miss the truth that it is also a responsibility.

As Christians we are at war with the world, at war with the flesh, at war with the devil.

He was a murderer from the beginning, and abode not in the truth, because there is no truth in him.
When he speaketh a lie, he speaketh of his own: for he is a liar, and the father of it.   John 8:44

At such a time as this, it isn't just about speaking lies, as much about living them: we allow false narratives to sway our thinking and our actions and our words.

As Christians we are strangers to the world, existing as aliens in the hostile environment of the world; we are marginalised by our trust in the truth of God's word; we are excluded by our unwillingness to conform to the enslavement of popular opinion.

If ye continue in my word, then are ye my disciples indeed: And ye shall know the truth, and the truth shall make you free. John 8:31,32

Our fight is not directed against the people who are recognised as the principle decision makers of this world. Our fight is directed against the one who is inspiring and leading them: the devil. And it is a fight to take back control of our minds from the captivity of lies, and to liberate ourselves with the weapon of truth, which is the word of God.

For the word of the LORD is right: and all his works are done in truth. Psalm 33:4

In the latter times some shall depart from the faith, giving heed to seducing spirits, and doctrines of devils; speaking lies in hypocrisy; having their conscience seared with a hot iron;

1 Timothy 4:1,2

This people draweth nigh
unto me with their mouth,
and honoureth me with their
lips; but their heart is
far from me.

But in vain they do worship
me, teaching for doctrines the
commandments of men.

Matthew 15:8,9

Awake, awake; put on thy strength

The Church should be an unyielding body that defends Truth.
The church should not compromise its integrity with a world that denies the truth.
The church should hold fast to the word of God, and boldly declare the truth.
Because, if not the church, then who?

Be ye not unequally yoked together with unbelievers: for what fellowship hath righteousness with unrighteousness? and what communion hath light with darkness?
2 Corinthians 6:14

COVID vaccines are a public health experiment using crudely-tested and improperly-licensed technology that is so unsafe that the only way manufacturers would agree to supply them was if governments shielded them from liability.

To subdue people who refuse to conform, governments across the world introduced the tactics of totalitarianism: fear-driven propaganda and censorship; the manipulation of science and statistics; the suppression of debate, and the condemnation of opposition. Psychological warfare techniques have been deployed for controlling official narratives, silencing dissent, and overplaying the pandemic to promote mandatory mass vaccinations.

Totalitarianism: *A system of government in which the people have virtually no authority and the state wields absolute control; the political concept that the citizen should be totally subject to an absolute state authority.*

People are being coerced to accept vaccination: government is using threats of discrimination, job loss, banned from public transport, excluded from schools, parks, sports and entertainment venues, bars, restaurants, public sector employment, and healthcare.

Unvaccinated people experience exclusion, marginalisation, vilification, purges by social media and mainstream media, as well as threats of violence, incarceration, legal reprisals, and the deprivation of civil rights.

At such a time as this: where does the church stand?
At such a time as this: where does *your* church stand?
At such a time as this: where do you stand?

Why do the heathen rage, and the people imagine a vain thing?

> The kings of the earth set themselves, and the rulers take counsel together, against the Lord, and against his anointed, saying, Let us break their bands asunder, and cast away their cords from us.
>
> Psalm 2:1-3

Fiddling while Rome burns

I love Ireland: it is my home; but recently Northern Ireland where I live has been abused and corrupted by outside interference.

After generations of bloody conflict between Nationalists and Loyalists, a fragile sort of peace was established in 1998 that has allowed our children to grow up in a much more peaceful environment than the one that my generation experienced and considered normal.

According to the 1998 Good Friday Agreement (or, Belfast Agreement), as a citizen of Northern Ireland I enjoy the right to claim British nationality, and I enjoy the right to claim Irish nationality.

(Some might argue, the best of both worlds!)

However, due to a three-year huff by our political representatives (that resulted in none of us enjoying any sort of political representation from our local government), the British government quite openly established Brexit: The withdrawal of the United Kingdom from the European Union.

Brexit has been the most significant change to the status of Northern Ireland since the partition of Ireland 100 years ago. And all this happened while our elected leaders maintained their self-imposed impotence.

Previously I could be fully British, and I could be fully Irish.
Now, I am not quite British, and I am not quite Irish.
I am not quite out of the European Union; and not quite in it.
I am neither all here, nor all there!
Northern Ireland is neither red-white-and-blue, nor green-white-and-gold: it's all just sort of muddy.

Despite all the flag-waving, it is an accepted matter of fact that just another election or two, and the Nationalist voters will have procreated a majority over the less prolific Loyalist voters, and Northern Ireland will democratically move towards being a Province of Ireland again.
It's just matter of good breeding, I guess.

The point I want to illustrate here is that Northern Ireland became politically and economically disadvantaged in plain sight.
And despite reassurances from the British Prime Minister, the dogs in the street could see that the hard-won Good Friday Agreement was being torn up as Northern Ireland was used as a sacrificial pawn to gain a small advantage for English political and economic positioning.

Similarly, as governments impose ungodly mandates, if people can't realise that what is happening to their freedom, to their civil rights and to their democracy [in plain sight], the people will have no one to blame but themselves when their country ends up under marshal law that will make Stalin's USSR look like Disneyland.

And the church should be proactive [not passive] in the resistance of ungodly government mandates.

I am grateful for the Good Friday Agreement. I am pleased that my children have no firsthand knowledge of the violence and terror that was considered normal here for so long.

Perhaps the future state of Northern Ireland is inevitable?
But your state of conviction should not be in doubt when it comes to placing your trust.

Do you believe the word of God, or do you believe the conflicting information from the media and government spin-doctors?

Do you put your trust in facemasks and vaccines; or do you trust the established word of God?

Do you trust politicians and scientists who are clearly muddling their way through, while their multi-billionaire benefactors continue to benefit?

For when they say, Peace and safety; then sudden destruction cometh upon them, as travail upon a woman with child: and they shall not escape.
1 Thessalonians 5:3

And be not
conformed to this world:
but be ye transformed by the
renewal of your mind, that ye
may prove
what is that good,
and acceptable,
and perfect,
will of God

Romans 12:2

Forgers of lies, physicians of no value

The government and media are feeding us distorted facts and dangerous lies.

God gave the Ten Commandments to Moses, literally written in stone.

The commandments include: *Thou shalt not bear false witness against thy neighbour.*
Exodus 20:16

Notice that it doesn't just say, *Thou shalt not tell a lie.*

A more literal translation of the text might be: You must not testify falsely.

In a court of law this phrase could be interpreted as:

You must not mislead;

You must not distort the truth;

You must tell the truth, the whole truth, and nothing but the truth.

It is common knowledge that statistics are often used as a crafty method of twisting facts and figures to gain advantage and win arguments.

And crafty wordplay has become a political artform: politicians frequently avoid answering questions with a completely irrelevant or misleading reply. Many politicians even employ 'spin-doctors' whose specific responsibility is to make bad news appear good!

The government and the media continuously feed us the information that they want us to hear: they feed us negativity; they feed us doom and gloom; they feed us fear.

The official information for COVID-related deaths is not reliable.

Among others, I have spoken with a senior nurse who has worked on the COVID ward of a city hospital since March 2020. She is very distressed at the fact that people are dying of the usual causes (heart disease, dementia, diabetes, cancer, etc.), but the cause of death written on the death certificate is COVID.

I have spoken with a police officer who openly told me that he is responding to the highest reports of domestic abuse that they have ever experienced; I have spoken with an administrator from a women's refuge who told me that they are receiving the highest number of calls for help and re-homing than they have ever experienced; I have spoken with a manager of a food bank who exclaimed that they are simply overwhelmed by the recent unprecedented demand for help. Etc,...

It is clear that there is something very sinister happening at the highest levels of administration, over-emphasising COVID so that the very harmful results of government interference are covered up; and the only reason I can imagine why they would want to do this is to stimulate more fear, which will allow government to further increase its control over the population.

But ye are forgers of lies, ye are all physicians of no value. O that ye would altogether hold your peace! and it should be your wisdom. Job 13:4,5

It is discouraging to realise that so many pastors and ministers readily complied with the government strategy of fear: closing their places of worship, complying with the wearing of facemasks, and some even encouraging those they shepherd to get vaccinated.

Haven't they understood the message of freedom and empowerment of the New Testament that we enjoy through Jesus Christ?

I partly blame the worldly compliance of church leaders on the control that government has incrementally gained over them.

Most churches are now constituted organisations, which means they are legally obligated to answer to the standards dictated by non-Christian outsiders.

The UK government even controls most churches financially through the additional 25% Gift Aid that the government adds on top of member donations.

Many churches are registered as charities so that they can claim back 20% VAT on infrastructure spending.

Churches are insured for public liability, which gives non-Christians control over church activities, especially during times of government interference.

This is worldly control of the church.
It is no wonder that so many church leaders are conforming to the world: they have become legally obligated to conform to the world at the expense of the Kingdom of God.

What should be the Christian response?

Put on the whole armour of God, that ye may be able to stand against the wiles of the devil.
Ephesians 6:11

Without a doubt, lies are one of the primary weapons of the devil; he is the deceiver.

For we wrestle not against flesh and blood, but against principalities, against powers, against the rulers of the darkness of this world, against spiritual wickedness in high places.
Ephesians 6:12

Even the dogs in the street recognise that something very sinister is happening across the world: the over-reaction to the inflated COVID statistics, and the tragic repercussions of lockdowns, and the rushed rollout of ineffective vaccination programmes: there is spiritual wickedness at work at this time.

Wherefore take unto you the whole armour of God, that ye may be able to withstand in the evil day, and having done all, to stand.
Ephesians 6:13

It is obvious that politicians and scientists do not have all the answers: the only sure foundation of truth is found in God's word: only through Jesus Christ can we truly enjoy salvation, freedom, and empowerment.

Stand therefore, having your loins girt about with truth, and having on the breastplate of righteousness; And your feet shod with the preparation of the gospel of peace; Above all, taking the shield of faith, wherewith ye shall be able to quench all the fiery darts of the wicked. And take the helmet of salvation, and the sword of the Spirit, which is the word of God:
Ephesians 6:14-17

All of this armour of God is facing forward: We are to stand and face the enemy.
All of the armour of God is protective, except for the sword. The sword of the Spirit is the word of God.

Unlike the world, we do not fight fire with fire: We respond to lies with truth; we respond to hatred with love; we respond to curses with blessings; we respond to intolerance with patience; we respond to mockery and slander with silence; we respond to false accusations with the word of God.

Jesus said: If the world hate you, ye know that it hated me before it hated you.
If ye were of the world, the world would love his own: but because ye are not of the world, but I have chosen you out of the world, therefore the world hateth you. John 15:18,19

Open the eyes of your heart to the truth of what is happening to your family, to your neighbours, to your community, and to your nation.

How can a passive follower of Jesus claim to be a follower of Jesus. Ask yourself what it means to be a follower of Jesus. Ask yourself: what would Jesus do?

Would Jesus conform to the conspiracy of lies and misinformation that we are being fed by government and the media?

Be still: and meditate on what it means to follow Jesus.

And ask in prayer: That the God of our Lord Jesus Christ, the Father of glory, may give unto you the spirit of wisdom and revelation in the knowledge of him:

The eyes of your understanding being enlightened: that ye may know what is the hope of his calling, and what the riches of the glory of his inheritance in the saints,

And what is the exceeding greatness of his power to us-ward who believe, according to the working of his mighty power,

Which he wrought in Christ, when he raised him from the dead, and set him at his own right hand in the heavenly places,

Far above all principality, and power, and might, and dominion, and every name that is named, not only in this world, but also in that which is to come: Ephesians 1:17-21

When peace, like a river, attendeth my way,
When sorrows like sea billows roll;
Whatever my lot, Thou hast taught me to say,
It is well, it is well with my soul.

*It is well with my soul,
It is well, it is well with my soul.*

Though Satan should buffet,
Though trials should come,
Let this blest assurance control,
That Christ hath regarded my helpless estate,
And hath shed His own blood for my soul.

My sin, (oh, the bliss of this glorious thought!),
My sin, not in part but the whole,
Is nailed to the cross, and I bear it no more,
Praise the Lord, praise the Lord, O my soul!

For me, be it Christ, be it Christ hence to live:
If Jordan above me shall roll,
No pang shall be mine, for in death as in life
Thou wilt whisper Thy peace to my soul.

But, Lord, 'tis for Thee, for Thy coming we wait,
The sky, not the grave, is our goal;
Oh, trump of the angel! Oh, voice of the Lord!
Blessed hope, blessed rest of my soul!

And Lord, haste the day
When my faith shall be sight,
The clouds be rolled back as a scroll;
The trump shall resound,
And the Lord shall descend,
Even so, it is well with my soul.

It is Well with My Soul, by Horatio G Spafford, 1873

And from the days of
John the Baptist until
now the kingdom of heaven
suffereth violence,
and the violent
take it by force

Or: The realm of heaven's kingdom is bursting forth, and passionate people have taken hold of its power. [The Passion Translation]

Matthew 11:12

Neither cold nor hot

It is commonplace nowadays to see people spontaneously pause to reverently bow their head. But they are not praying: they are just enchanted by their mobile phone.

I see lots of young people with the knees torn through on their jeans. But their knees are not worn from praying: it's just a fashion thing, apparently.

The culture of this world has already infiltrated the Western church; worldliness has bled into the fellowship.
It can often be difficult to recognise the difference between the church and the world.
It can often be difficult to recognise the difference between a Christian and a non-believer.

I know thy works, that thou art neither cold nor hot: I would thou wert cold or hot.
So then because thou are lukewarm, and neither cold nor hot, I will spue thee out of my mouth.
Revelation 3:15,16

Churches are filled with people who believe in God, who sing songs about God, and who can perhaps recite long passages from God's word.

But going to church, believing in God, singing songs and reciting scripture does not make you a Christian.

Believing won't save you

Thou believest that there is one God; thou doest well: the devils also believe, and tremble. James 2:19

Jesus Christ is not of this world: he is a mystery, and he is a wonder, and he is beyond the comprehension of this world. And there is absolutely no way in which the standards of the world can compare with the perfect standards of Jesus Christ.

Yet, it is common to see a church were the influence of the world has already leeched a deep stain into the fabric of Christian worship: where performance has replaced worship; where the worshipers have been relegated to the passive role of observers and spectators.

There are more modern translations of the Bible available now than ever before; there are library-loads of books of Bible teaching; there are television and radio stations broadcasting Christian worship and chat all hours of the day and night; there are blizzards of booklets and tracts freely available.
Yet this generation appears to be the weakest group of Christians the world has ever seen.

What should we do?

Should we submit to the herd?
Should we surrender to the liberals?
Should we succumb to the dead church?
Should we simply join those who have chosen to walk in the faintest shadow of Christian living?

God forbid!

The world will always be a threat: sin, unbelief, media, celebrity, money, and ambition; however skilfully disguised, the influences of the world will always be a threat to the Christian soul.

However, the Bible plainly teaches us that we should forsake the world, and actively avoid being influenced by it: we should not be in bondage to the world.

Christian liberty is the freedom to live unhindered by the world.

Christian liberty is the: freedom from fear of government; freedom from fear of our sins; freedom from fear of the devil; freedom from fear of curses or superstitions; and freedom from religious traditions.
Christian liberty is the freedom to live in the Spirit, and to worship God in spirit and truth.

The world is conditioning Christians to accept what is wrong as good.

Sexual promiscuity, adultery, pornography, violence, murder, rape, war, revenge, overindulgence, and the culture of celebrity: this is accepted as mainstream entertainment in people's homes. And with this entertainment comes other ungodly influences: everything from evolution to sexual disorientation. And it is fed into our minds and into the minds of our children until it is accepted and normalised.

Woe unto them that call evil good, and good evil: that put darkness for light, and light for darkness: that put bitter for sweet, and sweet for bitter! Isaiah 5:20

Slaves to propaganda

Propaganda: *communication that is used to influence an audience to further an agenda; selectively presenting facts, ideas or statements that are false or exaggerated and that are spread with the intention to help a cause, a political leader, government agenda, etc.*

Conditioning the mind creates slaves who are unaware that they are being conditioned to slavery.

Harmful ideas are being drip-fed to the masses; and these ideas are being adopted and learnt, and accepted as justifiable.

People believe that what the world tells them is the truth, and they ignorantly accept it and comply. And it is done so craftily that people don't even realise that they have been conditioned; they don't realise that a manipulative mind is moulding their beliefs and their principles and their morals. The elite few who control the media are controlling the world.

Who shall you allow to control you?
Will it be politicians?

Will it be the news media?
Will it be film and television entertainment?
Will it be the popular opinion of social media?

Or will it be God?

Wherewithal shall a young man cleanse his way? by taking heed thereto according to thy word.
Psalm 119:9

Unless you are awakened, you will think the way the world thinks.
Unless you are awakened, you will value what the world values.
Unless you are awakened, you will love what the world loves.

And unless you are awakened, you will ignore what the world ignores.

Take up your cross

I enjoy fidelity and loyalty with my wife; but without love our marriage would be a hollow and unfulfilled relationship.

Similarly, a Christian may behave like a Christian, do good like a Christian, speak nicely like a Christian; but without love for God it can only remain a hollow and unfulfilled relationship.

If you accept the presence of God; if you acknowledge that God is the Creator; if you accept that Jesus is the Christ who came into the world to rescue us from our sins: **thou**

doest well: the devils also believe, and tremble.
James 2:19

If you believe who and what God is, but do not accept the salvation offered to you through the sacrificial death, burial and resurrection of Jesus Christ, you are in the same damned category as demons.

Though I speak with the tongues of men and of angels, and have not charity, I am become as sounding brass, or a tinkling cymbal.
1 Corinthians 13:1

What is it that you are trusting in, if you are not trusting in God?

Jesus told us to pick up our cross and follow; he told us to obey the commandments; he told us to repent; he told us to give up everything; he told us to die to the world.

Jesus taught us to love: Jesus taught us what love is, and what love does, and how love acts, and how love lives.

And after Jesus taught us about love, he willingly picked up his cross, carried it up Calvary's hill, and he became the very definition of love.

Greater love hath no man than this, that a man lay down his life for his friends.
John 15:13

complacency compromise compliance conformity & Christ

Be Thou my vision, O Lord of my heart;
Naught be all else to me, save that Thou art.
Thou my best thought, by day or by night,
Waking or sleeping, Thy presence my light.

Be Thou my wisdom, be Thou my true word;
I ever with thee, and Thou with me, Lord.
Born of thy love, Thy child may I be,
Thou in me dwelling and I one with Thee.

Be Thou my buckler, my sword for the fight.
Be Thou my dignity, Thou my delight,
Thou my soul's shelter, Thou my high tower.
Raise Thou me heavenward,
O Power of my power.

Riches I heed not, nor vain empty praise;
Thou mine inheritance, now and always.
Thou and Thou only, first in my heart,
Ruler of heaven,
my treasure thou art.

High King of heaven, when victory is won
May I reach heaven's joys,
O bright heaven's Sun!
Heart of my heart, whatever befall,
Still be my vision,
O Ruler of all.

Translated from old Gaelic by Mary E Byrne, 1905

Beware lest any man spoil you
through philosophy
and vain deceit,
after the tradition of men,
after the rudiments
of the world,
and not after Christ.

Colossians 2:8

Forsake the foolish

There is an astonishing lack of discernment described between King Hezekiah of Judah, and a gift-bearing prince of Babylon, (2 Kings chapter 20).

King Hezekiah had been gravely ill; his physicians had given him only days to live, but God healed Hezekiah and promised him another fifteen years of life and protection.

The King of Babylon had heard of Hezekiah's illness, and had sent his son with letters and a gift.

Hezekiah responded by giving the Babylonian entourage a guided tour: there was nothing in his palace or in all his kingdom that Hezekiah did not show them.

Because of this, Isaiah delivered a message to Hezekiah from God:

Behold, the days come, that all that is in thine house, and that which thy fathers have laid up in store unto this day, shall be carried into Babylon: nothing shall be left, saith the Lord.

And of thy sons that shall issue from thee, which thou shalt beget, shall they take away; and they shall be eunuchs in the palace of the king of Babylon. 2 Kings 20:17,18

Babylon represents worldliness: a place where man celebrates his own accomplishments: a place were there is no thought for God.
Hezekiah had opened his doors to unbelievers and revealed the riches that God had blessed him with.

But how can unbelievers grasp the concept of an unseen benevolent, gracious, loving God?
As Christians, we live as exiles in the worldly kingdom of Babylon.

Even today, unbelievers see Christians, and mock: Why go to church when you can take a nice walk, or go shopping?
What do they do in church anyway: sing a bunch of happy-clappy songs; listen to someone sermonising for half-an-hour; talk to an invisible person; perform some religious ritual; and all go home again until next Sunday!

What unbelievers see of Christians is a bunch of nice people, who have a nice social gathering once a week in their nice church building, (*government restrictions may apply*).

Unbelievers do not, and cannot, understand the personal passionate supernatural relationship between a heavenly Father and his beloved children.
Unbelievers can only understand what their natural senses allow them to understand; they

only understand what they can see or hear or feel or smell or taste.

These kindly Babylonian tourists who got a guided tour of King Hezekiah's wealth also only understood with their five natural senses, and failed to understand the wonderful supernatural relationship between the one true God and his chosen people.

King Hezekiah replied to Isaiah with words of selfishness intent:
Is it not good, if peace and truth be in my days?
2 Kings 20:19

(Paraphrased in modern lingo: *"I'm alright, Jack! That'll be someone else's problem"*)

When God had healed Hezekiah of his terminal illness and blessed him with another fifteen years of life and security, Hezekiah knew that he would be protected from the danger of any foreign threats; it might all go horribly wrong for the next generation, but for Hezekiah: he could eat, drink, and be merry.

Passivity

When government interferes with Christian beliefs and values and rituals, almost nothing happens; in fact when the government ordered a lock-down of churches in 2020, it wasn't the police or the army who locked shut the church doors: it was the church leaders.
Why was that?

Why should anyone take Christ seriously? In most cases people will have more reason to take Islam seriously, because Muslims demonstrate serious loyalty to their faith.

A Muslim who prays five times each day lying facedown on the floor is clearly taking his religion seriously.

On the other hand, a Christian who seldom prays (and rarely on his knees), who goes to a church that appears to be a social club, and who blends in with non-Christians to such an extent that they are indistinguishable: such a person clearly does not take his religion seriously.

Insult the name of Allah to a Muslim, and you could easily start a riot.

Insult the name of Jesus to a Christian, and chances are that he'll laugh along with the rest of the crowd.

Why is that?

And from the days of John the Baptist until now the kingdom of heaven suffereth violence, and the violent take it by force. Matthew 11:12

A loving and devoted faith is forceful and aggressive in its pursuit of God; it rejects everything that gets in the way or that does not come from God; it is violent in the spirit against complacency, compromise, and compliance to ungodly interference.

Because, without an aggressive and passionate love for God and the truth of his word, the church risks being diluted to nought in the secular apathy of the world.

Soldiers of Christ, arise,
and put your armour on
Strong in the strength which God supplies
through His eternal Son.
Strong in the Lord of Hosts
and in His mighty Power,
Who in the strength of Jesus trusts
is more than conqueror.

Stand then in his great might,
with all his strength endued;
But take, to arm you for the fight,
the panoply of God.
Leave no unguarded place,
no weakness of the soul;
Take every virtue, every grace,
and fortify the whole.

To keep your armour bright,
attend with constant care;
Still walking in your Captain's sight,
and watching unto prayer.
From strength to strength go on;
wrestle and fight and pray;
Tread all the powers of darkness down,
and win the well-fought day.

Soldiers of Christ Arise, by Charles Wesley 1749

But if not

Both sides of the next page is Psalm 91.
This is a powerful psalm that you can rip from this book to keep in your pocket, to help bolster your trust in God in times of trial.

He that dwelleth in the secret place of
the most High shall abide under the
shadow of the Almighty.
I will say of the LORD, He is my refuge
and my fortress: my God;
in him will I trust.
Surely he shall deliver thee from the
snare of the fowler, and from the
noisome pestilence.
He shall cover thee with his feathers,
and under his wings shalt thou trust:
his truth shall be
thy shield and buckler.
Thou shalt not be afraid for the terror
by night; nor for the arrow
that flieth by day;
Nor for the pestilence that walketh in
darkness; nor for the destruction that
wasteth at noonday.
A thousand shall fall at thy side, and ten
thousand at thy right hand;
but it shall not come nigh thee.
Only with thine eyes shalt thou
behold and see the
reward of the wicked.

Because thou hast made the LORD,
which is my refuge, even the most High,
thy habitation;
There shall no evil befall thee, neither
shall any plague come nigh
thy dwelling.
For he shall give his angels charge over
thee, to keep thee in all thy ways.
They shall bear thee up in their hands,
lest thou dash thy foot
against a stone.
Thou shalt tread upon the lion and adder: the young lion and the dragon shalt
thou trample under feet.

Because he hath set his love upon me,
therefore will I deliver him:
I will set him on high, because he hath
known my name.
He shall call upon me, and I will answer
him: I will be with him in trouble; I will
deliver him, and honour him.
With long life will I satisfy him,
and shew him my salvation.

Psalm 91

complacency compromise compliance conformity & Christ

Many shall be purified,
and made white, and tried;
but the wicked
shall do wickedly:
and none of the wicked
shall understand: but the
wise shall understand.

Daniel 12:10

But if not

This is one of those phrases from God's word that I cannot simply read past; it stops me, like I've walked into a glass wall.

But if not...

This phrase from chapter three of the Book of Daniel is profound in its context and relevance to us today.

King Nebuchadnezzar's armies had attacked and defeated the kingdom of Judah. Taken into Babylon as captives were the cream of Judean society: all the royal family, all the young people who were handsome and skilful and wise and clever.

Living as Judean captives and officials to King Nebuchadnezzar in Babylon were four Hebrews who each had Godly names:

Daniel (the LORD is my judge),
Hananiah (the LORD is gracious),
Mishael (who is what the LORD is?), and
Azariah (the LORD has helped).

However, in pagan Babylon they had been given pagan names that mocked their faith.

Daniel was given the name, Belteshazzar, (Beltis protect the king),
Hananiah was given the name Shadrach (command of the moon god Aku),
Mishael was given the name Meshach (who is as Aku is?),
Azariah was given the name Abednego (slave of Nabu, the god of literacy and wisdom).

These pagan names were probably given to try to separate them from the religion and traditions of their homeland, in a vain hope to indoctrinate them into the ways of this new pagan world.

After their name changes, the very next thing that is recorded is Daniel's refusal to defile himself with the food and wine that was provided for them from the king's table.

You might be thinking, 'What's the harm in eating the same food as the king?' And the bible story does not explain 'why not', but the point is this: Daniel realised in his heart that it was not right – so he and his colleagues refused this fine food and wine.

This is the first real test of character and loyalty to God: these young men were offered the very finest food and wine, and all they had to do was what everyone else was doing: eat, drink, and enjoy it.

The temptation to follow the crowd may have been convincing, and the act seemingly harmless; but these young men steadfastly refused to comply, preferring to eat vegetables with plain water.

Sometimes, we don't know why something is wrong because it is not obviously wrong.
Rarely will a wrong thing have a warning label on it.
But a small still voice in your heart may be telling you it is wrong, and urges you to resist the temptation to yield or comply.
Perhaps this is how you feel when you are expected to wear a facemask or line up for vaccination?

As a reward for their loyalty, God gave them knowledge and skill in all learning and wisdom: and Daniel had understanding in all visions and dreams. Daniel 1:17

And in all matters of wisdom and understanding, that the king enquired of them, he found them to be ten times better than all the magicians and astrologers that were in his realm. Daniel 1:20

King Nebuchadnezzar remains one of the wealthiest and most powerful kings in all of human history.
As you might expect from a megalomaniac, Nebuchadnezzar created an awesome statue of gold that stood nearly 90-feet tall; at the given sound, the people of all races and nations and languages were ordered to bow down obediently before this great golden idol.

As an incentive to comply, anyone who refused to obey this law would be burnt alive in a blazing furnace.

Shadrach, Meshach, and Abednego steadfastly refused to compromise their loyalty to the one true God: they refused to bow to this hollow man-made idol.

Some of the king's astrologers snitched, and eagerly told their king:

There are certain Jews whom thou hast set over the affairs of the province of Babylon, Shadrach, Meshach, and Abednego; these men, O king, have not regarded thee: they serve not thy gods, nor worship the golden image which thou hast set up. Then Nebuchadnezzar in his rage and fury commanded to bring Shadrach, Meshach, and Abednego. Then they brought these men before the king. Daniel 3:12,13 KJV

Given the alternative, what would you do?
Would you be obedient to an ungodly instruction?
Or, would you disobey the ungodly command and be thrown into a furnace to be burnt alive?
Shadrach, Meshach, and Abednego chose to be thrown into the furnace rather than comply with this ungodly command.

If it be so, our God whom we serve is able to deliver us from the burning fiery furnace, and he will deliver us out of thine hand, O king.

> But if not, be it known unto thee, O king, that we will not serve thy gods, nor worship the golden image which thou hast set up.
> Daniel 3:17,18

But if not,...

Even if God would not move to save them from the furnace, these three men were prepared to die rather than conform and comply to an ungodly act that demonstrated a compromise of their trust in God.
These men put their whole trust in God.
Even at the threat of death they refused to obey this powerful king's decree.
They could have pretended to bow down, (perhaps to tie their shoelaces or scratch their ankles), but they steadfastly refused to conform in any way.

They did not have a guarantee from God that they would be protected from harm.

They had not received a message from an angel, or a revelation in a dream.

But, they were fully prepared to trust God, even if it meant suffering a cruel death.

Why should I comply with an official decree when I know that it conflicts with God's word?
Are you prepared to steadfastly refuse to comply with ungodly instructions, even if the alternative is dreadful?

Do, or die

Let me bring this ancient Bible story up to date with a notable incident that happened in Egypt, April 2017.

A small convoy of Christians was travelling on a pilgrimage to a monastery in the desert when they were attacked by about ten fundamentalist Muslims.

The attackers shot at the minibus containing children, killing at least six, including a four-year old, and a two-year old.

A truck containing workmen travelling to the monastery was also targeted, killing at least eight of the men.

Gunmen entered the other bus, killing several of the men in their seats, before handing out Islamist leaflets to the women and girls.

The remaining men and boys were forced to exit the bus and kneel in the sand where they were asked to recite the Shahada [an Islamic oath]; and were executed one-by-one as they refused.

This incident is not isolated: in the same month Muslims bombed two Christian churches in Egypt, killing forty-five people and injuring at least 125 others.
And in Egypt the following year, this bus attack was repeated on another Christian pilgrimage, killing twelve.

On average, every day of 2021, thirteen Christians were killed because of their faith. Every day, twelve churches or Christian buildings were attacked. And every day twelve Christians were unjustly arrested or imprisoned, and another five Christians were abducted, because of their faith.

As of 2021, there were 309,000,000 Christians living in places with very high or extreme levels of persecution; and another 31,000,000 Christians could be added to this list from the twenty-four nations that fall just outside the top fifty most Christian-intolerant nations.

COVID had been used as a catalyst for Christian persecution in many nations: relief discrimination, forced conversion, increased surveillance, and censorship.

Christians live in constant risk of being imprisoned, tortured, beaten, raped, and executed, (beheaded, shot, stoned, crucified or hanged from streetlights); their churches are demolished, and their property is burnt.

And yet, Christians in these places continue to secretly gather to meet in the name of Jesus Christ, to worship the one true God.

How does this compare to your commitment to God?

Before turning this page, ask yourself this:

But if God does not save me from persecution, am I steadfastly prepared to be loyal unto him?

Even if it means being killed?

Blessed is the man that
walketh not in the
counsel of the ungodly,
nor standeth in the
way of sinners,
nor sitteth in the seat
of the scornful.

But his delight is in the law of
the LORD;
and in his law doth he
meditate day and night.

Psalm 1:1,2

Conspiracy Theologist

I prefer to encourage, than discourage.

However, I am aware that many church leaders are openly embarrassing people who have refused the COVID vaccination.

Is it not wicked, even persecution, to condemn a person for standing on their convictions to trust in God's word?

Such convicted people have been labelled 'conspiracy theorists.'

Am I a conspiracy theorist?

YES, I am!

I believe in the great conspiracy whose origins are clearly recorded in Genesis chapter 3 when man was deceived by the serpent, and everything went dreadfully wrong.

Because of his finished work (his death, burial and resurrection), Jesus is the only person through whom we can overcome the powers of wickedness and the affects of this broken world.

The word of God explains the things that must take place prior to the return of Jesus and the Judgement.

And sinister things are coming together in the world right now that can be interpreted as shadows of the last days that are described in the Old and New Testaments of God's word.

Conspiracy belongs to the devil Truth belongs to Jesus

People who are following the herd and promoting vaccination are the deluded conspiracy theorists – hook, line and sinker.

I can't understand how a church leader can consider the vaccination to be anything other than sinister when they know that these vaccinations are manufactured using the substance from aborted innocent children.

Jesus sent the Holy Ghost to influence us in our correct decision-making; yet many people are being led by the lies of the world, the media, distorted news, and general ignorance; Christians are following the popular opinion of the herd when they should be following the still small voice of God speaking into their heart.

It appears that church leaders have been targeted by the sinister forces of the world; some have been made dangerously ill with COVID, and are now being used as willing servants to spread fear and obedience to vaccination.

How can a person teach others to trust in God and the truth of his covering protection – but then encourage others to queue up to receive an ungodly vaccination?

Either God's word is truth, or God is a liar!

If God is a liar, then there is no salvation, no hope, and Jesus could have saved himself a lot of bother.

But, **GOD'S WORD IS TRUTH**.

And ye shall know the truth, and the truth shall set you free. John 8:32

Spot the conspiracy theorist

Put it this way: next time you're in a supermarket, take a good look around you. Who among all the shoppers look like they are living free:
- The ones mumbling behind facemasks?
- Or, the few without facemasks?

And, who among all the shoppers look like they are conspiracy theorists:
- The ones who drove alone in their car wearing a facemask, who sprayed their hands with alcohol at the door, and who keep six feet away from all the other shoppers?
- Or the few who carry on without regard to fear and conformity?

Live by faith, or die by doubt

I had arranged to buy a load of old chairs from a church in Belfast recently. Once we had agreed the deal, I asked the minister how things had been, what with government restrictions and fearfulness of members.

He said that things were beginning to get back to some form of normality. So, I cheekily asked him how he equated Daniel's attitude to conforming to totalitarianism with ours?

Here's a quick reminder:
A decree had been established by unalterable law that for the next thirty days any person who worshipped anyone, divine or human – other than King Darius – would be thrown into the den of lions.

Daniel completely ignored this decree,
He went into his house: and his windows being opened in his chamber toward Jerusalem, he kneeled upon his knees three times a day, and prayed, and gave thanks before his God, as he did aforetime. Daniel 6:10

Daniel knew that the penalty for disobeying the law was to be cast into the den of lions. But Daniel refused to compromise – he refused to conform to a worldly law that came between him and his God.
Daniel would rather be torn apart and eaten alive by lions than compromise his worship of the one true God.
Daniel continued to worship God three times each day, just as before.

Our churches ceased gathering to worship just once each week, even when the risk would have been a minor penalty in comparison.

I plainly told the minister that I have a firm and steadfast trust in the truth of God's word – God's word says that he will protect me, and I firmly believe this.

The minister raised an eyebrow, smiled and inquired, "So, if you threw yourself out this upstairs window would you expect God to protect you from injury?"

I didn't answer his question.
It would have been wrong to embarrass him.
Because a similar question was once asked of Jesus:

Then the devil taketh him up into the holy city, and setteth him on a pinnacle of the temple, and saith unto him, If thou be the Son of God, cast thyself down: for it is written, He shall give his angels charge concerning thee: and in their hands they shall bear thee up, lest at any time thou dash thy foot against a stone.

Jesus said unto him, It is written again, Thou shalt not tempt the Lord thy God.
(Matthew 4:5-7)

A few minutes later while carrying batches of chairs downstairs to the van, I pointed up to a Boys' Brigade poster on the wall, and exclaimed, "That's what I'm taking about."

The minister looked at me quizzically!

Quoting the BB standard, I asked, *"Will your anchor drift, or firm remain?"*

I can understand the difficult position church leaders are in, but where do they draw the line?

To his credit I have to say that this city-centre church leader wasn't wearing a facemask, and he greeted me and parted company with a firm and friendly handshake, which is a rare thing these days.

Conformity is easy.
Compromise is simple.

Standing on conviction can be a difficult trial.

Will your anchor hold in the storms of life,
When the clouds unfold their
wings of strife?
When the strong tides lift,
and the cables strain,
Will your anchor drift or firm remain?

We have an anchor that keeps the soul
Steadfast and sure while the billows roll,
Fastened to the Rock which cannot move,
Grounded firm and deep
in the Saviour's love.

It is safely moored,
'twill the storm withstand,
For 'tis well secured by the Saviour's hand;
And the cables passed from
His heart to mine,
Can defy the blast, through strength divine.

It will firmly hold in the straits of fear,
When the breakers have
told the reef is near;
Though the tempest rave
and the wild winds blow,
Not an angry wave shall our bark overflow.

It will surely hold in the floods of death,
When the waters cold chill our latest breath;
On the rising tide it can never fail,
While our hopes abide within the veil.

Will Your Anchor Hold, by Priscilla Owens   1838-1921

But if not

For God hath not given us the spirit of fear;
but of power,
and of love,
and of a sound mind.

2 Timothy 1:7

Complacency

It was my own fault that I was almost mugged in an underground carpark in Shanghai; and I am still embarrassed by my foolishness.

It was a familiar commute for me back then, and my guard was down; weary and impatient from my long journey from Belfast to Heathrow to Pudong, once I had beaten my way through the crowds exiting the airport, my heart sank when I realised that the jostling mob of people outside were, like me, waiting for a taxi. So, when an enthusiastic voice offered to take me to a taxi waiting in the car park, I just followed him, like a sheep trotting off to a barbeque.

Complacency can be a very dangerous thing. I don't like crowds, and my Mandarin is ropey at best, so this helpful little man seemed like a good idea at the time; until he got into the back seat of the taxi beside me and subtly slipped his hand inside his jacket breast pocket!

Often, when we put our trust in others, it can be too late to do anything by the time we realise that we are in actual danger.

I thank God for his loving protection and the calm that he blessed me with in that interesting confrontation; I am so grateful that my assailants were more foolish than me, and I actually managed to negotiate my way out of their trap at only a small financial cost. (In different circumstances I could have lost my life; my coffin could have been a dumpster, and my grave the city dump.)

Thank you, Father.

Perhaps one of the reasons why churches in the West have so readily bowed to government COVID restrictions is because we have it so easy here; most churches have become dangerously complacent.

Most people don't realise that the social-distancing, mask-wearing, and vaccine passports are the thin edge of a deep wedge that has already brought church and state into direct conflict.

When I worked in China, government surveillance was obvious: I knew my phone could be tracked and used as a microphone to monitor conversations (even if I had turned it off); my daily movements were known, CCTV cameras were everywhere; and if there was an incident or accident nearby, uniformed officials seemed to appear from out of nowhere.

I enjoyed very little privacy, and (despite this mugging attempt) I generally felt very safe.

In the years since I last worked in China, surveillance has become much more sophisticated, and China is employing advanced surveillance technology to monitor and protect its citizens from 'threats'.

And that's the slogan: *It's for your own safety.*

Communism *versus* Christians

One of the 'threats' that the Chinese Communist Party are coming down hard on just now is Christianity.

In 2020 there were:-

- Nine documented church demolitions carried out by the Chinese Communist Party, affecting over 5,000 attendees, (I expect that there were many other church demolitions that were not documented).
- The Chinese Communist Party persecuted all known house churches; and police summonsed for questioning the leader of every main church.
- All churches, even small house churches, must fly the Chinese flag.
- All churches must sing patriotic Chinese songs at services.
- And all preaching must conform to Chinese Communist Party ideology.

Chinese Communist Party authorities invade Christians' homes, raid family gatherings, and interfere with parenting decisions.

There are numerous reports of Christians being sued by the authorities for home-schooling children, or for sending them to church-run schools.

Chinese state schools are teaching children that Christianity is an evil cult; children in state schools are taught to oppose religion, and report family members who are Christians.

What can we learn from China?

The Chinese Communist Party may not appear to affect you directly; however, the enforced lockdowns, mandatory social distancing and facemasks policies adopted by Western governments are all control tactics that were successfully enforced by the Chinese Communist Party, (I know, because I experienced their heavy-handed tactics firsthand while working in China during their 2002 SARS outbreak).

Two key lessons we can learn from what is happening in China:

- Christianity is an acknowledged threat in China because Christianity is a movement, (similar to the 1st Century ekklesia of the New Testament). (Christianity in China is less of an organisation, like the organised churches in the West today.)

- And we need to recognise that the government COVID restrictions that have been imposed on Western church gatherings since 2020 are the thin edge of a destructive wedge similar to that being used by the Chinese Communist Party to subdue Christians.

Consider your brothers- and sisters-in-Christ who are being persecuted for their faith in China.

If they are being persecuted for their love of Jesus Christ, they must be doing something RIGHT !

And despite how difficult it must be to endure persecution for their love and loyalty to Jesus, I encourage them to re-double their efforts, and be blessed.

Blessed are they which are persecuted for righteousness' sake: for theirs is the kingdom of heaven. Matthew 5:10

When we have a choice between doing what government tells us to do, or what God's word tells us to do: we need to choose to follow God, (not man).

"Oh! But my church leaders say we should wear facemasks, we should sit apart, we should avoid handshakes and hugs, we should be vaccinated."

Many churches are more focused on getting bums on seats and crating converts, than developing and nurturing proactive disciples.

They would happily explain conforming to the world as "loving and protecting our neighbour," regardless of how this conforming to the world conflicts with God's Word.

And be not conformed to this world: but be ye transformed by the renewing of your mind to know what is that good, and acceptable, and perfect will of God. Romans 12:2

Don't just put on the life-jacket of salvation and climb aboard the ark to wait for heaven: Get out of the boat, and do what Jesus told you to do, always keeping our eyes upon him: because, The harvest truly is plenteous, but the labourers are few. Matthew 9:37

Jesus is not just your Saviour
Jesus is Lord of your life.
Jesus is your King

Jesus is: above all principality, and power, and dominion, and every name that is named not only in this world but also in that which is to come, and hath put all things under his feet, and gave him to be the head over all things to the church, which is his body, the fullness of him that filleth all in all. Ephesians 1:21-23

Do you truly understand who Jesus is to you?

Do you realise the superiority of Jesus over every area of your life?

We are often taught what Jesus has done for us, and will do for us. But we should actively be focussing on what we can do for Jesus.

It shouldn't matter what your president or prime minister, or pastor is telling you to do:
If what your president or prime minister or pastor tells you to do conflicts with the Word of God: they are wrong.
If they tell you to stop meeting for fellowship: they are wrong.
If they say you should refrain from worshipping God in song: they are wrong.
If they say that you should hide your face behind a mask when you are healthy: they are wrong.
If they say that you should go get vaccinated: THEY ARE WRONG!

His watchmen are blind: they are all ignorant, they are dumb dogs, they cannot bark: sleeping, lying down, loving slumber. Isaiah 56:10

The sinister vaccines developed to 'protect' us from COVID have been manufactured using cells from aborted human beings.

God's word is clear: killing innocent human life is wrong: abortion is the killing of innocent human life: abortion is wrong.

Because abortion is wrong, hoping to benefit from a drug developed using an aborted human is wrong: these vaccines are wrong.

China may be thousands of miles away: a far away totalitarian state with a different culture and society and language and all the rest of it. But, the persecution of Christians that is happening openly in China today could easily and very quickly be the new normal for comfy conforming Christians in the West tomorrow.

Wake up!

Acceptability of homosexuality and transgenderism is being taught as part of the mainstream school curriculum.
Same-sex marriage is protected by law and accepted by society [and some churches].
Evolution is the accepted origin of all life on earth, including humans.
Abortion is offered as a means of birth-control.
I cannot go on radio or television and state that, *"Jesus Christ is the Way, the Truth, and the Life."* No! I have to qualify such a statement with, *"According to the Bible,…"*

Now, don't get me wrong here: Jesus came to offer the only true hope of salvation to homosexual abortionist atheists, just the same as he did for you and me; people just need to realise what is being offered to them, and receive their salvation.
But, the point is this: incrementally, Christians are being marginalised.

Incrementally, Christians are being conditioned to accept and conform to the mainstream thinking of the world.

Incrementally, things that God hates are becoming normalised and justifiable.

We are all being conditioned to conform by the cleverly skewed information we are being fed by government, news and media.

Let me illustrate this with a simple metaphor: If your church was a boat, would it be a sound boat? Because all boats let in water one way or another, either by wave action, or rain storms, or a leaky hull! But your boat can only be fit for purpose while it floats; the more water that infiltrates your boat, the less safe your boat becomes. You need to protect the integrity of your boat: you need to identify where the water is getting in, bale it out, and plug the leaks.

Do not compromise your faith

If a person in authority tells you to do something that conflicts with the Word of God, that person is wrong, and you should refuse to comply; you should refuse to compromise.

And he shall set the sheep on his right hand, but the goats on the left. Matthew 25:33

Pray for our persecuted brothers- and sisters-in-Christ who are living in fear of government persecution across the world.

Pray that they are invigorated in the power and protection and provision of God.

And pray that you will also remain strong, refusing to compromise your faith in God's power and protection and provision for you.

As the last days approach, expect your faith to be tested, expect your trust in God to be challenged. Be prepared: arm yourself with God's word: if you don't have some scripture committed to heart, then keep a miniature copy of the Bible in your pocket.

(On pages 69/70 and 123/124 of this book there are two encouraging Bible chapters that you can rip out and keep in your pocket.)

God's word is the sword of the Spirit, your only sure defence against the trials that must come before God's ultimate plan can be fulfilled.

Blessed are they which are persecuted for righteousness' sake: for theirs is the kingdom of heaven.

Blessed are ye, when men shall revile you, and persecute you, and shall say all manner of evil against you falsely, for my sake.

Rejoice, and be exceeding glad: for great is your reward in heaven: for so persecuted they the prophets which were before you.

Ye are the salt of the earth: but if the salt have lost his savour, wherewith shall it be salted? it is thenceforth good for nothing, but to be cast out, and to be trodden under foot of men.
(Matthew 5:10-13

Conforming to the world: perhaps this could be likened to being, trodden under foot of men.

Would you agree?

"No compromise with evil"
Shall be our battle cry,
For God and right must conquer,
And sin and wrong must die;
Unflinching we are standing
uncompromisingly,
Beneath the flag of holiness
Forever we will be.

No compromise, no compromise,
This shall be our battle cry,
For God and right we will boldly fight,
We will keep the standard high.

No compromise with error,
For Bible truth we stand,
Let none remove the landmarks
Erected by God's hand;
With loyalty our watchword
And faith in Christ our stay,
We'll bravely storm the forts of sin
And through Him win the day.

No compromise with worldliness,
No yielding to the wrong,
No lowering the standard
That's stood through ages long;
With Jesus as our leader,
His Spirit as our guide,
We'll firmly stand for righteousness
Whatever may betide.

No Compromise, by Haldor Lillenas, 1913

And such as do wickedly against the covenant shall he corrupt by flatteries: but the people that do know their God shall be strong, and do exploits.

Daniel 11:32

Superficial faith

Shepherding was an amazing privilege.

The first day I started work as a farm labourer I was asked to go check the sheep with the other lad who would show me what to do and what to look for.

As soon as I hopped the gate, the whole hundred-or-so sheep panicked and took off to the far corner where they huddled in a fearful rotating mass of wool and bulging eyes.

I checked the sheep most every day after that for the next seven years while I was there. Within the first week the sheep became more familiar with me, and I was easily able to count them and check them for signs of problems that might need sorted. After a short while I could walk through the flock, and they would completely ignore me! I would have to push them to their feet to check for limps or other issues.

They became very familiar and trusting of me; and likewise, I became very familiar with them.

I knew which ones had a tendency to wander or get their stupid head stuck in the wire fence; I knew the ones that needed more attention; and I could pick out one of our lost sheep from a neighbouring flock, just by looking at her face. I could even lead the sheep from one field and down the road to the next field simply by calling them, and they would follow.

At lambing time, this trust between the shepherd and ewe is essential. Labour may be complicated: a lamb may be stuck, or the wrong way round inside, and I'd have to settle the ewe so she would allow me to manipulate the lamb within her womb (with my winter-cold hands).

I am the good shepherd, and I know my sheep, and am known of mine. John 10:14

I do not consider myself an adequate preacher or teacher, (I write words more eloquently than I speak them); I have never been asked to pastor anyone; after a season of assisting with corporate praise, I don't think I've been missed; and I do not consider my brief contribution as a deacon to have been remarkable.

But I do know about shepherding.

I know that the shepherd is completely trusted by his flock; I know that the shepherd is fully accountable for the health and safety of each individual sheep in his flock; I know that in times of trouble, or storms, or flood, or snow, or danger, it is the shepherd, and the shepherd only, that the sheep look to for their security.

Similarly, we are the sheep, and Jesus is the good Shepherd: he is the very best Shepherd.

However, there is a problem with a lot of his sheep (that's us!).

We do not completely trust in our good Shepherd; we do not entrust our safety to our good Shepherd; and in times of trouble or crisis, we do not look to our good Shepherd for our safety and security.

Ironically, we instinctively turn to another one of us for help!

As a former shepherd's hired hand, it is a ridiculous thought to me that sheep might attempt to provide for their own health and provision and comfort and safety and security.

Putting your trust in man is like a sheep putting its trust in another sheep: it's plain foolishness.

Any shepherd can tell you that sheep are defenceless and incapable of looking after themselves. When troubles come, without their shepherd they will just panic and follow each other round and round in bleating circles.

The LORD is my shepherd: I shall not want.

He maketh me to lie down in green pastures: he leadeth me beside the still waters.

He restoreth my soul: he leadeth me in the paths of righteousness for his name's sake.

Yea, though I walk through the valley of the shadow of death, I shall fear no evil: for thou art with me: thy rod and staff they comfort me.
Psalm 23:1-4

In God we trust?

The man of superficial faith will declare his belief in God, but avoid getting himself into a predicament where his future must depend upon his belief being true.

The man of superficial faith will always provide himself with alternative means of escape if his faith is ever put to the test.

But what is needed at such a time as this is a body of Christians who are prepared to trust God now, as they know they must trust him at the last day; because the time is coming when health and wealth and friends and hiding places will all be swept away, and we shall have nothing to trust upon except the truth of God.

The church has lost its authority to change the world because in complacency the church has been corrupted by compromised by worldly and ungodly influences.

You cannot have authority over the enemy you are sleeping with.
When you are in agreement with your enemy you lose your authority over him.

The world has recently become so strongly opposed against the purposes of God that compliance and complacency will lead many Christians to be swept away in the sinister tides of deception, delusion, and enslavement.

The LORD is my rock, and my fortress, and my deliverer: my God, my strength, in whom I will trust; my buckler, and the horn of my salvation, and my high tower.   Psalm 18:2

Compromised

As I write this, I regret that I am no longer a member of my local church fellowship. After a brief dialogue with my pastor I resigned my membership. This is quite a turnaround from being a deacon and leading from the front every week. I had resigned from the church leadership team a few weeks prior to the 2020 lockdown. And following the closing of the church doors, I struggled to accept compliance with worldly interference. I recognised that my restlessness risked causing discord among brethren, and I solemnly stepped away.

Based on God's word, I believe that it is unacceptable to pretend that gathering in socially distanced seating can be described as freedom or fellowship.
Based on God's word, I believe that healthy people wearing a facemask during fellowship symbolises fear and conformity to the world.
Based on God's word, I believe that accepting vaccination is turning my back on God's promises of protection.
And based on God's word, I cannot conceive of any excuse for a follower of Jesus Christ to knowingly accept a vaccine developed using the substance from a murdered innocent human life.

To compromise my trust in God's word and accept such conformity to the world does not reflect the freedoms that Jesus won for us.

Rather, conforming to such things is living in bondage to the world.

Now we have received, not the spirit of the world, but the spirit which is of God; that we might know the things that are freely given to us of God. 1 Corinthians 2:12

The world has been living in end times for almost 2,000 years. I don't know when it will all conclude; however, I recognise that sinister things are building up in the world right now that can be closely interpreted as signs of the last days that are described in the Old and New testaments of God's word.

All I know for sure is that we are another day closer to the return of Jesus Christ, and the Judgement.

Now is not a time to start compromising.

At its heart, compromise is about self-preservation.
How can God reward compromise?
This doesn't mean that God doesn't love you, or that he is mad at you, or will punish you. But how can God intervene in your life without your permission? faith-filled obedience without compromise gives God permission to intervene.

If you want God to intervene on your behalf, you need to obey God. You need to start living by faith, without compromise.
If you want to walk on water, you have to get out of the boat.

"But I might drown!"
Just keep your eyes on Jesus, the author and the finisher of your faith, and don't be distracted by the boisterous wind and waves.
God rewards people who stand on their conviction.

Behold, to obey is better than sacrifice, and to hearken than the fat of rams.
For rebellion is as the sin of witchcraft, and stubbornness is as iniquity and idolatry.
1 Samuel 15:22-23

As I write this, I no longer enjoy the fellowship of my local church. But I firmly declare my love for my Father, and affirm my membership of the ekklesia of Jesus Christ, the global Kingdom movement of followers of Jesus.
And no one can take this membership away from me without my permission.

My God: in him will I trust.   Psalm 91:2

And the LORD said unto
Moses, Wherefore criest thou
unto me?
Speak unto the children of
Israel, that they go forward:

Exodus 14:1

Revive as the corn, and grow as the vine

Church is becoming more dilute in effectiveness, and marginalised by society.
Surrendering to government mandates made things worse: making church life a shadow of the freedom and empowerment that we should be living in, through Christ.

Perhaps now is the time for a reboot.
Perhaps it is time to reintroduce the ekklesia that Jesus spoke about.
Because church as we know it today is not the kind of church that we read about in the New Testament.

Why did Jesus use the Greek word, ekklesia?
Why didn't Jesus use the word for a temple, or synagogue?

Our church organisations are built on the systems and rituals of a temple. But this is not what Jesus asked us to build.

The two times that Jesus spoke about church in the Bible, he only used the word ekklesia, (Matthew 16:18, and Matthew 18:17).

When Paul wrote about church, he also only used the word ekklesia.
Same with John, and James, and Peter: ekklesia.

When King James commissioned an English translation of the Bible, I believe that he used his regal authority to influence the translators to tweak the liberating meaning of the Greek word 'ekklesia' and interpret it as the more passive word 'church'.
I believe that King James imposed this interpretation to avoid a Christian threat to his regal authority: because an ekklesia could have threatened the English monarchy.
And following suit, several subsequent Bible translations have also adopted 'church' for the word 'ekklesia'.

What was an ekklesia?

An ekklesia was an entirely non-religious assembly.
An ekklesia was an assembly of citizens of the democratic city-states of Greece.
These assemblies were active across the breadth of influence of the democracy of Greece (which, in New Testament times, included the area we refer to as the Holy Land).
These ekklesia existed hundreds of years before the birth of Jesus.
The ekklesia was responsible for things like debating municipal matters, electing officials

to office, (it was a representative assembly with powers similar to our magistrate courts and local borough councils today, I guess, but less exclusive).

But the ekklesia had nothing to do with religion.

You can read a dramatic description of a city ekklesia at work in the book of Acts chapter 19, verses 23 to 41.

Here, the effectiveness of Paul's preaching caused a bit of a riot, and the local assembly of the city (the ekklesia) rushed to the theatre to noisily debate what they should do with the Christians who were threatening the prosperity of their city and their famous pagan temple.

Here, 'ekklesia' is used for this secular assembly twice: in verses 23, and 41.

Why did Jesus use the term ekklesia?

Jesus is a revolutionary leader!

And be not conformed to this world: but be ye transformed by the renewing of your mind, that ye may prove what is that good, and acceptable, and perfect, will of God. Romans 12:2

If Jesus had wanted his followers to use a temple or synagogue as an organisational template for his disciples to duplicate, he would not have used 'ekklesia'.

What did the early church [the ekklesia] do so right, that the present-day church does so badly? Because the early ekklesia clearly worked very effectively.

Acts 2:41 describes three thousand people gladly becoming followers of Jesus in just one day!

Verily, verily, I say unto you, He that believeth in me, the works that I do shall he do also; and greater works than these shall he do: because I go unto my Father. John 14:12

As Jesus had predicted, his disciples were emulating him, and through God's power they were achieving very similar results in miracles and healing, (see: Acts 2:43-47; 5:14-16; 8:12; 13:44,49; 17:4; 18:8 and; 19:11,20).

The Christian ekklesia in Ephesus became so successful that the people of that city burnt all of their pagan scrolls and artefacts, enthusiastically destroying many very valuable items.

Within the lifetime of Paul, the Christian ekklesia won over the Roman region of Asia, and established proactive centres of Christian influence across Greece and Italy and North Africa and Ethiopia.

How is any of this effectiveness replicated by what we nowadays recognise as 'church'?

Jesus said that, *The law and the prophets were until John: since that time the kingdom of God is preached, and every man presseth into it.*
Luke 16:16

Forgive me, but I don't recognise much pressing in just now! We are not just short of disciples: in fact most churches I know of have been struggling to fill seats for decades.

The harvest truly is plenteous, but the labourers are few: Matthew 9:37

Perhaps it's time for a rethink.
Perhaps it's time for a reboot.
Perhaps it's time to reconsider ekklesia?

Think about it:
The early followers of Jesus didn't have bicycles or cars or trucks or trains or aeroplanes,...
They didn't have satellite communications, or mobile phones, or digital television and radio,...
They didn't have SatNav, or social media, or Youtube, or Zoom,...

They had ekklesia.

The ekklesia quickly achieved extensive growth, so much so that Paul was even planning a mission to Spain, which was at the edge of the civilised world in those days!

Even with all of our modern technological advantages, our churches struggle to get the bloke next door to take notice of the gospel message – a message of truth that should leave him utterly overwhelmed with joy!

If Jesus is so irresistible, and the gospel message is such good news, could the refusal of people to receive it be the result of us doing and preaching something less?

To see the results that the church has not yet seen, perhaps the church needs to do what it has not yet done; because if the church keeps doing what they've always done, they'll keep getting what they've already got, (which is a faint shadow of what the original ekklesia was achieving).

What was the ekklesia doing so right?
What are our churches doing so wrong?

I do not claim to have all the answers.
I am aware that Roman Emperor Constantine may have had a very negative influence on the Christian church/ekklesia, imposing such things as worship on a Sunday (the same day on which Constantine worshipped his sun god); and giving over pagan temples to the Christians for their gatherings, (which naturally became ritualised and conformed to old religious practices, and dependant on income to meet the escalating overheads of such buildings and institutions); and he instituted a religious hierarchy that was ultimately led by a pope.

People will not be drawn to the Kingdom by a church building, or a church organisation, or a church hierarchy.
People will be drawn by witnessing God's Kingdom as a living and proactive and integral part the common workplace and the marketplace and the government, and in every aspect of society and business and decision-making.

You and I, we are ekklesia: we are pastors, we are ministers, we are preachers, we are healers, we are whatever God has purposed us to be in his Kingdom.

We are ambassadors of Jesus Christ commissioned and authorised to continue the work that he started here 2000 years ago.

The devil was defeated through the death, burial and resurrection of Jesus Christ.
The devil is finished.

However, the devil and his demons are still active: they are losers, fighting a battle in a war that they lost when Jesus Christ took back at the cross everything that the devil won from humanity in the Garden of Eden.
The devil is a loser, but the devil is still active as a master of lies and deception, and I count him responsible for the fracturing of Christian believers into a multitude of factions and denominations, trying his best to divide and conquer.

(There is an old joke about a new arrival to heaven being given a guided tour, and asked to silently creep past the door of a Christian sect that is particularly strict; the guide explaining that, "They think they're the only ones here!")

We are often too busy justifying our way of doing church, and criticising others' ways, so much so that we often forget who the real enemy actually is!

Distracted, we frequently fail to make ourselves usable by God for the purposes that he designed us for in his Kingdom.

Personally, I don't care what denomination you claim to be: if you truly believe that Jesus Christ is the Way and the Truth and the Life, I embrace you as my brother- or sister-in-Christ.

Such a time as this

Perhaps now is time, (during this season of fear, and government interference of church), for a reboot, so that we can realise what Jesus asked us to do in his Kingdom.

Perhaps now is the time to re-read the New Testament in the light of the original meaning of the word ekklesia.

Perhaps now is the time to re-assess the effectiveness of our present-day methods of mission work and local outreach that simply are not as effective as they should be, (and falling well sort of the effectiveness that is described in the book of Acts).

Perhaps now is the time to re-imagine what true fellowship is in terms of a worldwide Christian belief and solidarity of purpose through Jesus.

Perhaps now is the time to realise that it isn't enough to be Christian once a week, but that every moment of every day we each need to be a living expression of Jesus Christ: active ambassadors of his Kingdom: bringing light to the darkness of this world that Jesus poured out his blood to save.

And perhaps now is the time to really live the instructions that Jesus gave his followers before he ascended to God's right hand in heaven:

Afterward he [Jesus] appeared unto the eleven as they sat at meat, and upbraided them with their unbelief and hardness of heart, because they believed not them which had seen him after he was risen.

And he said unto them, Go ye into all the world, and preach the gospel to every creature.

He that believeth and is baptized shall be saved; but he that believeth not shall be damned.

And these signs shall follow them that believe; In my name shall they cast out devils; they shall speak with new tongues;

They shall take up serpents; and if they drink any deadly thing, it shall not hurt them; they shall lay hands on the sick, and they shall recover.

So then after the Lord had spoken unto them, he was received up into heaven, and sat on the right hand of God.

And they went forth, and preached every where, the Lord working with them, and confirming the word with signs following.

Amen.

Mark 16:14-20

> Thy word is a lamp
> unto my feet,
> and a light
> unto my path.

Psalm 119:105

Bold as a lion

I don't want to criticise.
I want to encourage.
But it is difficult, because when most churches gather on Sundays they are operating under the controls and restrictions of ungodly government interference.
Isn't such behaviour perpetuating the climate of fear, (while claiming faith in words and song)?

A double-minded man is unstable in all his ways.
James 1:8

For me, to conform to social distancing, mask-wearing, and waving a vaccine passport at church would equate to ripping out several chapters from the Word of God.

I was laughed at in my work recently.
I am a manager, and I asked if I could pay for photocopying some private papers: the PA scoffed at me and told me to just take it. But this is the point: whether it is a sheet of plain paper, or a large packet of money, it doesn't make any difference: taking something

that doesn't belong to you is wrong, and even taking something as valueless as a sheet of paper is compromising your integrity.

Similarly, to claim the words of faith in God, but yet conforming to social-distancing and mask-wearing and vaccination seems to me to be openly compromising our trust in God's numerous promises of protection.

I admit that sometimes I might be a bit bold with my Father's promises of protection. I was getting a new back tyre fitted to my bike recently; it's a big powerful bike, but I was just wearing normal working clothes, no gloves, no boots, no protective clothing, just an open-faced helmet to keep me legal.

Another biker arrived and dismounted, pulled off his gloves, plucked his head from a full-face helmet, unpeeled his heavily armoured leather jacket, and began struggling out of his back protector harness; he stood beside me, perspiring profusely inside his armoured leather trousers and boots.

I thought our comparison was funny!

I am aware of how vulnerable I am on a bike; I have dealt with the mess of a crash; I know how things can go very wrong very quickly. But I pondered as I roared away with my new tyre: Am I perceived as being reckless, not only with my commute, but with my trust in God in relation to global health scares?

My God: in him will I trust. Psalm 91:2

Even with the best intentions, a facemask is a symbol of fear and conformity.

For God hath not given us the spirit of fear; but of power, and of love, and of a sound mind.
Timothy 1:7

As brothers- and sisters-in-Christ, greeting one another with a handshake or an embrace should be second nature.

Greet ye one another with an holy kiss. 1 Corinthians 16:20, 2 Corinthians 13:12, 1 Thessalonians 5:26
Greet ye one another with a kiss of charity.
1 Peter 5:14

Being asked to show a vaccine passport before entering church simply screams against everything that fellowship ought to be.

And be not conformed to this world; but be ye transformed by the renewal of your mind, that ye may prove what is that good, and acceptable, and perfect will of God. Romans 12:2

If ye were of the world, the world would love his own: but because ye are not of the world, but I have chosen you out of the world, therefore the world hateth you. John 15:19

You could reason that these words of Jesus imply that if we are not hated by the world, we must be doing something wrong!
I will not compromise my trust in God and the finished the work of Jesus Christ.
I will happily be mocked.
I will gladly be hated.

And I will faithfully rest in my God whom I love and trust.

Both sides of the next page is Isaiah chapter 6
This is a powerful and inspiring chapter that you can rip from this book to keep in your pocket to help bolster your trust in God in times of trial.

The first half of this chapter describes the amazing glory and holiness of God.
The second half illustrates how God is always in ultimate control, even when things appear to be hopeless.

In the year that king Uzziah died I saw also
the LORD sitting upon a throne, high and lifted
up, and his train filled the temple.
Above it stood the seraphims:
each one had six wings; with twain he
covered his face, and with twain he covered his
feet, and with twain he did fly.

And one cried unto another, and said,
**Holy, holy, holy, is the LORD of hosts: the
whole earth is full of his glory.**
And the posts of the door moved at the voice of
him that cried, and the house
was filled with smoke.

Then said I, **Woe is me! for I am undone;
because I am a man of unclean lips, and I
dwell in the midst of a people of unclean
lips: for mine eyes have seen the King,
the LORD of hosts.**

Then flew one of the seraphims unto me,
having a live coal in his hand, which he had taken
with the tongs from off the altar:
And he laid it upon my mouth, and said,
**Lo, this hath touched thy lips; and thine
iniquity is taken away,
and thy sin purged.**

Also I heard the voice of the LORD, saying, **Whom
shall I send,
and who will go for us?**

Then said I, **Here am I; send me.**

And he said,
Go, and tell this people,
Hear ye indeed, but understand not;
and see ye indeed, but perceive not.

Make the heart of this people fat, and
make their ears heavy, and shut their
eyes; lest they see with their eyes, and
hear with their ears, and understand with
their heart, and convert,
and be healed.

Then said I,
Lord, how long?

And he answered,
Until the cities be wasted without
inhabitant, and the houses without man,
and the land be utterly desolate,
And the LORD have removed men far away,
and there be a great forsaking in the
midst of the land.

But yet in it shall be a tenth,
and it shall return, and shall be eaten:
as a teil tree, and as an oak,
whose substance is in them, when they
cast their leaves: so the holy seed shall be
the substance thereof.

Isaiah chapter 6

complacency compromise compliance conformity & Christ

Know ye not that
ye are the temple of God, and
that the Spirit of God dwelleth in you?
If any man defile the temple of
God, him shall God
destroy; for the temple of God
is holy,
which temple ye are.

1 Corinthians 3:16,17

A form of godliness

Avoid profane and vain babblings, and oppositions of science falsely so called: which some professing have erred concerning the faith.
1 Timothy 6:20,21

There is ungodly reasoning being spread by many church leaders that the vaccination is acceptable for Christians because God has inspired scientists with the ability to create vaccines!
I believe this is wicked lies and nonsense.
I believe that they are taking God's name in vain to suggest that the vaccine inventors were inspired by God: because God does not approve the killing of innocent human lives whose substance was used to develop these vaccines.

Shall the throne of iniquity have fellowship with thee, which frameth mischief by a law? They gather themselves together against the soul of the righteous, and condemn the innocent blood.
Psalm 94:20,21

Are the pro-vaccine church leaders suggesting that, because Goliath had superior skills and superior armour and superior weapons and superior strength, that David should have just accepted defeat?

Then said David to the Philistine, Thou comest to me with a sword, and with a spear, and with a shield. but I come to thee in the name of the LORD of hosts, the God of the armies of Israel, whom thou hast defied. 1 Samuel 17:45

Are the pro-vaccine church leaders suggesting that, King Asa should have submitted to the far superior armies that combined to attack him with chariots and horsemen?

Were not the Ethiopians and the Lubims a huge host, with very many chariots and horsemen? yet, because thou didst rely on the Lord, he delivered them into thine hand.
2 Chronicles 16:8

Are the pro-vaccine church leaders suggesting that, feeding over five-thousand people with just five loaves and two fish would require very very big loaves and a couple of whales?

And they that had eaten were about five thousand men, beside women and children.
Matthew 14:21

We need to put our whole trust in God, not man.

We do not need to insure our faith with an ungodly vaccination, (as if God's promises of protection toward us are bedtime fairy tales).

To those pro-vaccine church leaders, be warned: *They that observe lying vanities forsake their own mercy.* Jonah 2:8

To confused and disappointed Christians who have been encouraged by their church leaders to accept the vaccines, or who have been offered no scriptural advice on the matter:
This know also, that in the last days perilous times shall come. For men shall be lovers of their own selves..... having a form of godliness, but denying the power thereof: from such turn away.
2 Timothy 3:1,2,5

I am deeply discouraged by pro-vaccine church leaders. And I am discouraged by church leaders who do not offer any godly direction or advice in respect of the vaccine.
How can a person claim to trust in God, but yet agree to accept such a sinister vaccine, like an insurance policy in case God's busy or doesn't really exist?

Many pastors have destroyed my vineyard, they have trodden my portion under foot, they have made my pleasant portion a desolate wilderness.
Jeremiah 12:10

If you are resisting pro-vaccine advice from your church leaders; if you are being pressurised, mocked, ridiculed, excluded: know that you are not alone.

Yea, and all that will live godly in Christ Jesus shall suffer persecution. 2 Timothy 3:12

There is a hymn by Jim Cowan, the words of which are appropriate for these times:

> When it's all been said and done,
> There is just one thing that matters
> Did I do my best to live for truth?
> Did I live my life for you?

To live for truth means to live not by lies. To willingly accept a vaccination created using the substance from a murdered innocent child, is not living for truth.

And when it is a proven fact that the vaccines and boosters do not work, but are in fact harming more people than they protect, to accept such a substance is to live by lies.

For we must all appear before the judgement seat of Christ: that every one may receive the things done in his body, according to that he hath done, whether it be good or bad.
2 Corinthians 5:10

What you can rest your trust in is far superior to an ungodly vaccination.
You have the blood of Jesus Christ.

I stand amazed in the presence
Of Jesus, the Nazarene,
And wonder how he could love me,
A sinner, condemned, unclean.

How marvellous, how wonderful!
And my song shall ever be:
How marvellous, how wonderful
Is my Saviour's love for me!

He took my sins and my sorrows;
He made them his very own;
He bore the burden to Calvary
And suffered and died alone.

When with the ransomed in glory
His face I at last shall see,
'Twill be my joy through the ages
To sing of his love for me.

I Stand Amazed, by Charles H Gabriel, 1856-1932

Let them alone:
they be blind leaders
of the blind.
And if the blind
lead the blind,
both shall fall
into the ditch.

Matthew 15:14

Asa, and trust

Meditating on the debate about vaccination, my mind is continually drawn to the reign of King Asa of Judah, (2 Chronicles chapters 14 to16).

King Asa made a lot of positive changes as soon as he began to rule Judah. He ordered the complete destruction of pagan shrines and altars, and the smashing of pagan symbols.
This spring-clean was pleasing and good in the sight of God, and the people of Judah were blessed.

Then, an Ethiopian army of 1,000,000 warriors with 300 chariots attacked Judah.
King Asa's combined strength was only 580,000 warriors. However, Asa put his trust in God, and the Ethiopian army was crushed; the army of Judah carried away a vast amount of plunder in the wake of the retreating Ethiopian hoard.

Because they recognised God's favour over them, the people of Judah made a promise to

continually seek the Lord God with all their heart and soul.
And God responded to their commitment to him by blessing the land with peace.
There was no more war until the 35th year of King Asa's reign.
Then, Israel invaded Judah.

In response to this aggression, King Asa took the silver and gold from the temple and palace treasuries to pay a bribe to King Ben-hadad who was ruling Damascus, to the north of Israel.
King Asa paid King Ben-hadad to invade Israel, thereby successfully distracting Israel from their attack on Judah.
However, as a result of King Asa's ungodly alliance with King Ben-hadad, he was rebuked by a messenger of God who told him that if he had put his trust in God instead of man, with God as their strength Judah would have easily defeated Israel, and would also have destroyed the armies of King Ben-hadad.

As a result of seeking strength in man instead of God, the kingdom of Judah did not enjoy peace, and was consequently continually at war with its neighbours.

Did you see what just happened there?

King Asa did not put his trust in God, as he had done when he was invaded by the much larger and better-equipped Ethiopian army.
King Asa put his trust in purchasing the military might of another king.
Why would he do that? especially after the promise that he and his people had previously

committed to, to continually seek and honour God!

And then, four years later, King Asa took a severe disease in his feet.
And again, instead of turning to God for his help and healing, Asa only turned to his physicians.

Yet in his disease he sought not to the LORD, but to the physicians. 2 Chronicles 16:12

King Asa suffered this disease for three years before he died of its consequences.

Are you like King Asa?

We can start our relationship with God with great enthusiasm, and realise wonderful benefits and blessings.
We can openly proclaim our faith in the death, burial and resurrection of Jesus, and be publicly baptised to demonstrate our obedience to God and his word.
We truly enjoy living in the blessings of God.
But then something scary happens!
And we look to the world for a solution, even after we have enjoyed the real benefits of a strong relationship with God.
And then we have a health-scare!
And again, we look to the world for protection, like we never knew God, like we never really believed his truth about his healing and protection over us.

I don't know why King Asa appears to have completely forgotten about his relationship with God.
King Asa seemed to do everything right.

And then he just did everything wrong!
And he paid the ultimate consequence.
Even if a vaccine was not manufactured using the substance of an aborted human being, my strongest argument for not accepting a vaccination is that I would be following in the foolish footsteps of King Asa, which led to his destruction.

You either put your whole trust in God, or you don't!

God isn't just some sort of lucky charm that you keep in a dusty drawer for emergencies: God is your constant loving Father.

Do you want to enjoy the peace and blessings that a relationship with God will bring to your life?
Or, do you want to rest your hope on the man-made short-term solutions of this world?

If the pandemic has taught us anything, it is the fact that our politicians and scientists do not have all the answers.

I give it to you on the highest possible authority that the word of God does have all the answers.

Before you consider conforming to the world, consider the blessings that God has offered you in his word, and ask yourself:
Do I trust man before God?
Or, do I trust God before man?

Come thou fount of every blessing,
Tune my heart to sing Thy grace;
Streams of mercy, never ceasing
Call for songs of loudest praise.

Here I raise my Ebenezer,
Hither by Thy help I've come;
And I hope by Thy good pleasure,
Safely to arrive at home.

Jesus sought me when a stranger,
Wandering from the fold of God;
He, to rescue me from danger,
Interposed His precious blood.

Oh, to grace how great a debtor,
Daily I'm constrained to be!
Let Thy grace, Lord, like a fetter,
Bind my wandering heart to Thee

Prone to wander, Lord, I feel it;
Prone to leave the God I love;
Here's my heart, oh, take and seal it,
Seal it for Thy courts above.

Come Thou Fount, by Rev. R Robinson 1758

Keep that which is committed to thy trust, avoiding profane and vain babblings, and oppositions of science falsely so called, which some professing have erred concerning the faith.

1 Timothy 6:20,21

Is God pro-choice?

Yes, God has given you a choice:
I have set before you life and death, blessing and cursing: therefore choose life, that both thou and thy seed may live. Deuteronomy 30:19

It's called free will:
With God,
Or, without him.

Many people consider Northern Ireland to be living in the dark ages when it comes to abortion.
By means of the interference and imposition of the British government, (while our local politicians continued with their childish three-year huff), abortions became legal in Northern Ireland in March 2020. Even so, things have moved very slowly: Amnesty International openly criticised the provision of abortion services, and the Northern Ireland Human Rights Commission launched legal action over the commissioning delay.

The Secretary of State for Northern Ireland stated that he wants a renewed focus on, "securing the abortion services that women and girls are entitled to." He said, "We should take our obligations on this issue incredibly seriously – it is a human right to be able to access quality healthcare."

He failed to mention the human right of access to quality healthcare for the innocent unborn child.

Another issue in the area of abortion is related to vaccines.

The majority of vaccines that are being rolled out across the world in response to COVID have used cells from aborted human beings in their manufacture and testing.

By accepting one of these vaccines you are hoping to profit from the death of an innocent human life.

Abortion is a subject that some people get rather excited about.

What does God say about abortion?

Abortion clinics were not a thing back when the Bible was written, but there is plenty of scripture to support the fact that destroying unborn human life is very wrong.

The Bible actually offers the unborn child protection under the law:

If an unborn child was killed, the person responsible would be punished as a murderer:

When men strive together and hit a pregnant woman, so that her children come out, but there is no harm, the one who hit her shall surely be fined, as the woman's husband shall impose on

him, and he shall pay as the judges determine. But if there is harm, then you shall pay life for life, eye for eye, tooth for tooth, hand for hand, foot for foot, burn for burn, wound for wound, stripe for stripe. Exodus 21:22-25

Unborn human life is precious.

Before I formed thee in the belly I knew thee: Jeremiah 1:5

But when it pleased God, who separated me from my mother's womb, and called me by his grace. Galatians 1:15

For thou hast possessed my reigns: thou hast covered me in my mother's womb.
My substance was not hid from thee, when I was made in secret, and curiously wrought in the lowest parts of the earth. Thine eyes did see my substance, yet being unperfect: and in thy book all my members were written, which in continuance were fashioned, when as yet there were none of them. Psalm 139:13,15,16

Thine hands have made me and fashioned me together round about: Job 10:8

Thus said the LORD that made thee, and formed thee from the womb, Isaiah 44:2

Did not he that made me in the womb make him? and did not one fashion us in the womb? Job 31:15

Behold, children are an heritage from the LORD, the fruit of the womb is a reward. Psalm 127:3

Moreover thou hast taken thy sons and thy daughters, whom thou hast borne to me, and these hast thou sacrificed unto them to be devoured. Is this of thy whoredoms a small matter, that thou hast slain my children, and delivered them to cause them to pass through the fire for them? Ezekiel 16:20,21

Cursed be he that taketh reward to slay an innocent person. Deuteronomy 27:25

Because he slew me not from the womb; or that my mother might have been my grave, and her womb to be always great with me. Jeremiah 20:17

I will not turn away the punishment thereof; because they have ripped up the women with child in Gilead. Amos 1:13

Should I have been aborted?

(My brother would probably say, Yes.)
The sexual relationship between my natural parents was illegal under the laws of the land, (and illegal under the Old Testament law – see Leviticus 18:15, and 20:12).
My parent's relationship was wrong.
My conception was shameful.
My existence could have humiliated my natural parents.
My natural parents went to great lengths to hide me and have me privately adopted.
I was a secret that they each took to their graves.

But it wasn't my fault!
I was, and remain, completely innocent of my natural parents' errors.
Did I deserve to be killed for my natural parents' mistakes?

Sometimes I take my life for granted!
I admit that I am occasionally reckless with my safety. But according to God's word, he has a purpose for me to fulfil.
And I shall continue to strive to make myself usable for his sake.

Having made known unto us the mystery of his will, according to his good pleasure which he hath purposed in himself:
That in the dispensation of the fulness of times he might gather together in one all things in Christ, both which are in heaven, and which are on earth; even in him:
In whom also we have obtained an inheritance, being predestinated according to the purpose of him who worketh all things after the counsel of his own will:
That we should be to the praise of his glory, who first trusted in Christ.
Ephesians 1:9-12

Ye therefore, beloved, seeing ye know these things before, beware lest ye also, being led away with the error of the wicked, fall from your own stedfastness.

2 Peter 3:17

A foot out of joint

Many Christians allow themselves to be suppressed by the devil; they live life on a level that is way below what is available to them through Jesus.

In fact, many of these people talk about the devil more than they talk about Jesus:
Every time they complain about bad luck, they are acknowledging the devil.
Every time they complain about being ill or depressed, they are acknowledging the devil.
Every time they speak negatively about a situation, they are acknowledging the devil.

And when people acknowledge the affects of devil, they risk empowering him in their lives.

Be sober, be vigilant: because your adversary the devil, as a roaring lion, walketh about, seeking whom he may devour:
1 Peter 5:8

Too often we give God our leftovers: the tired remains of our day; the residue of our income; and a half-hearted effort of our talents.

God gave the world his only begotten son.
Jesus gave up his perfect life, so that whosoever believes in him should not perish, but have everlasting life.

Herein is our love made perfect, that we may have boldness in the day of judgement: because as he is, so are we in this world. 1 John 4:17

A time of testing is coming, even a time of painful persecution; and lukewarm Christians will not survive with their faith intact.
We need to recognise how many of the world's values have been absorbed into Christian life and practice. We need to realise how the ways of the world conflict with what Jesus expects of his disciples, and seriously question ourselves:

Are we just admirers of Jesus?
Or, are we his followers?

Jesus called us to share in his Passion, to take up our cross. And if you are not committed to standing firm upon the truth of God's word, you are at risk of drifting away in the lukewarm tide of submission.

You have a choice:
Live by faith;
Or, die by doubt.

Confidence in an unfaithful man in time of trouble is like a broken tooth, and a foot out of joint. Proverbs 25:19

An unfaithful man is not someone you can rely upon in times of trouble: as soon as he is put under pressure, he will fail.

Strength in truth

I do not like being mocked for speaking truth.
I do not enjoy being rejected for my belief.
It hurts.
I have been attacked verbally, and spiritually, which has often manifested painfully and physically. I recently suffered a particularly deep and personal rejection that still has me a bit bewildered.
My reaction to such attacks and rejections?

Bring it on!

Because if speaking the truth in love brings me into direct conflict against principalities, and powers, and the rulers of the darkness of this world, and spiritual wickedness in high places: Then I know that I am doing something right.

And I'm going to keep doing it.
Because I'd rather wear out than go rusty.

Standing alone with God, you will always be in the majority.

He that justifieth the wicked, and he that condemneth the just, even they both are abomination to the LORD. Proverbs 17:15

The definition of 'abomination' is a thing that causes disgust or loathing.
Why would anyone want to be considered an abomination to God?
If you are at the receiving end of pressure to get vaccinated, if you are being emotionally blackmailed by your family and friends and colleagues, if you are being banned or discriminated or persecuted: Be blessed!

Blessed are they which are persecuted for righteousness' sake: Matthew 5:10

Trust in God's promises of protection that cover you. And know that, (despite how corrupt and crazy and chaotic this world may appear), God remains in ultimate control.

Peace I leave with you, my peace I give unto to you: not as the world giveth, give I unto you. Let not your heart be troubled, neither be afraid.
John 14:27

Before the throne of God above
I have a strong and perfect plea;
A great High Priest whose name is Love,
Who ever lives and pleads for me.
My name is graven on his hands,
My name is written on his heart.
I know that while in heaven he stands
No tongue can bid me thence depart,
No tongue can bid me thence depart.

When Satan tempts me to despair
And tells me of the guilt within,
Upward I look and see him there
Who made an end of all my sin.
Because the sinless Saviour died,
My sinful soul is counted free;
For God the just is satisfied
To look on him and pardon me,
To look on him and pardon me.

Behold him there, the risen Lamb,
My perfect, spotless righteousness,
The great unchangeable I AM,
The King of glory and of grace.
At one with him, I cannot die;
My soul is purchased by his blood.
My life is hid with Christ on high,
With Christ my Saviour and my God,
With Christ my Saviour and my God.

Before the Throne of God Above,
by Charitie Lees Bancroft, 1860

Let no man deceive himself.
If any man among you
seemeth to be wise in this
world, let him become a fool,
that he may be wise.
For the wisdom of this world
is foolishness with God.
For it is written,
He taketh the wise in their
own craftiness.

1 Corinthians 3:18,19

Days of Noah

But as the days of Noah were, so shall also the coming of the Son of man be.
For as in the days that were before the flood they were eating and drinking, marrying and giving in marriage, until the day that Noe entered the ark.
(Matthew 24:37,38

Eating, drinking, marrying and planning their future: seems like a normal kind of lifestyle with nothing remarkable to comment upon.

Except for the very obvious fact that Noah had been building an enormous ship for about 100 years! Everyone must have known about Noah and his ridiculous ark that he was building where there was no body of water to float it on.

Noah must have been a joke to everyone! Noah must have been considered a complete fool by the world.

This know also, that in the last days perilous times shall come. For men shall be lovers of their own selves, covetous, boasters, proud, blasphemers, disobedient to parents, unthankful, unholy, without natural affection, trucebreakers, false accusers, incontinent, fierce, despisers of those that are good, traitors, heady, highminded, lovers of pleasure more than lovers of God: having a form of godliness, but denying the power thereof: from such turn away. 2 Timothy 3:1-5

Grasping what feels good, instead of what is good, isn't good.
This generation more than any other is continually beset by the world in all five senses.

When I used to work abroad for long periods in the busyness and bustle of America or China, coming home was always so exciting. That Belfast departure lounge at Heathrow was wonderful to me because, even if I had to wait all day for my flight, I was only ever a one-hour flight away from home. And driving home from the airport late at night, I'd stop by the peaceful shores of Strangford Lough: the silence broken only by the lapping water, and above me the big black sky punctuated with a vivid myriad of stars; and I could breath again, fresh clean air refreshed my sullied lungs.
After a prolonged assault on my senses, (the perpetual noise and pollution and filth and confusion of the industrial cities where I worked), finally I could enjoy uninterrupted peacefulness, and realise God.

The heavens declare the glory of God: and the firmament sheweth his handiwork. Psalm 19:1

My point is this: if you struggle to realise the presence of God in the commotion and busyness of the rat race, but can easily realise God's presence in the peace and calm of his creation: spend less time enduring the man-made world, and spend more time enveloped in the peace and magnificence of God's creation.

Realising and enjoying the presence of God by being surrounded by the peace of his creation isn't my idea: Jesus retreated up a mountain, or into the wilderness to spend time with his Father. However, I guess Jesus knew that finding a convenient mountain or a wilderness wasn't going to be practical for a lot of people, so he advised that we find solitude in the next best place.

But thou, when thou prayest, enter into thy closet, and when thou hast shut thy door, pray to thy Father which is in secret: and thy Father which seeth in secret shall reward thee openly.
(Matthew 6:6

In my lifetime I have witnessed a secular revolution. I admit that the Council chaining-up the playpark swings on Sundays was a bit extreme when I was a kid; but the moral compass has swung so far now that almost anything is acceptable these days.

But, wherever we are, we are called to be ambassadors of Jesus Christ.
It is our duty to speak out for God's truth when it is attacked.

You may be labelled a prude for avoiding entertainment or speech or activities that promote immorality; you may be labelled a fool for believing in creation; you may be labelled homophobic for rejecting homosexuality; you may be labelled anti-feminist for rejecting abortion; and you may be labelled intolerant for professing the lordship of Jesus over your life.

And this is where passionate Christians are at greater risk in these times: because the church is fractured, because fellowship is broken, because divisions caused by government interference of the church has led to Christians [like me] departing from fellowships. Which means that without the support of one another, we have become weaker and more vulnerable.

We need other Christians with whom we can share encouragement, share struggles, and share victories.

And let us consider one another to provoke unto love and to good works: Not forsaking the assembling of ourselves together, as the manner of some is: but exhorting one another: and so much the more, as ye see the day approaching.
Hebrews 10:24,25

Decade after decade past, and the people watched and mocked as Noah continued to build his ark
Noah continued to warn the people.
Noah continued faithfully and passionately as a preacher of righteousness.

And the people shrugged their shoulders, and shook their heads with a mocking smirk.
And all the while nothing happened: no downpour, no flood, nothing that might cause them to consider climbing aboard that boat to remain safe.
The people just carried on living life as normal, and planning their future.

Until it was too late.

Can you recognise a climate of change?

But if the watchman
see the sword come,
and blow not the trumpet,
and the people be not warned;
if the sword come,
and take any person
from among them, he is taken
away in his iniquity;

but his blood will I require at
the watchman's hand.

Ezekiel 33:6

God forbid

If you have already conformed and complied and queued to receive this sinister vaccine, where do you stand with God?

In your naivety or foolishness or fear, if you have submitted to follow the advice of man, and complied with vaccination, is God mad with you?

If my child did something against my will, I would be disappointed; but they will always remain my child.

Salvation is not dependant upon abstaining from vaccination. God's gift of forgiveness is entirely dependant upon your acceptance of the perfect blood sacrifice of Jesus Christ who accepted the punishment for your sins.

Unto him that loved us, and washed us from our sins in his own blood. And hath made us kings and priests unto God and his Father; to him be glory and dominion for ever and ever. Amen
Revelation 1:5,6

It is impossible to be blameless of sin without accepting Jesus as your personal saviour. Whether you do it, or say it, or even think it: if it is a sinful thing that you do or say or think: that is sin.

For whosoever shall keep the whole law, and yet offend in one point, he is guilty of all. James 2:10

There is so much more to being a Christian than just climbing aboard the ark of salvation and waiting to drift to the heavenly shore; there is so much more, and if you want to walk on water you'll need to get out of the boat.

And these signs shall follow them that believe: In my name shall they cast out devils; they shall speak in new tongues; they shall take up serpents; and if they drink any deadly thing, it shall not hurt them; and they shall lay hands on the sick, and they shall recover. Mark 16:17,18

But what if you accept the vaccine because you were fear-driven by the onslaught of negative propaganda? What if you gave in to accepting a vaccine that is manufactured using the substance from aborted humans, knowing that it is wrong, but hoping that God will forgive you, (because that's what God does, doesn't he?)

What shall we say then? Shall we continue in sin, that grace may abound? God forbid. How shall we, that are dead to sin, live any longer therein? Romans 6:1,2

God calls us to separate ourselves from the godless spirit of the age, the spirit of Babylon that is dominating our culture.

Come out of her, my people, that ye be not partakers of her sins, and that ye receive not her plagues. Revelation 18:4

But many Christians are ignoring this warning; many Christians are attempting to maintain a dual citizenship with God's Kingdom and Babylon, which Paul teaches us is impossible:

For what fellowship hath righteousness with lawlessness? and what communion hath light with darkness? And what concord hath Christ with Belial? or what part hath he that believes with an infidel? And what agreement hath the temple of God with idols? for ye are the temple of the Living God. 2 Corinthians 6:14-16

If you have naively accepted the sinister COVID vaccinations, the only suggestion I can offer is to get down on your knees in shame and repentance, and ask God for his forgiveness and for his protection over you from the adverse effects of these sinister drugs that have now become indelibly intermingled with your blood.

Convicted of what?

If Christianity became illegal, there wouldn't be enough evidence to arrest many Christians.

And all that live godly in Christ Jesus shall suffer persecution. 2 Timothy 3:12

I could argue that if we aren't suffering persecution, perhaps we aren't living godly lives!
Fear of man and fear of persecution stop most people; most people are too timid or too weak to suffer persecution; they value the praises of man more than the praises of God.

If you take a moral stand on social issues, immoral people will criticise you; your morality will condemn them, and they will attack you in an attempt to make themselves look good.

But they measuring themselves by themselves, and comparing themselves among themselves, are not wise. 2 Corinthians 10:12

If you are afraid to speak out for Jesus, if you are afraid to stand up for God's truth, it's because you value the opinions and acceptance of others more than you value God. If you don't want to expose yourself to the possibility of being ridiculed or criticised or rejected, you haven't placed a proper value on God.

This lack of courage will leave you wide open: all the devil needs to do is put you in yet another situation where you will again compromise your trust, incrementally disconnecting you from God.

Finally, my brethren, be strong in the Lord, and in the power of his might. Put on the whole armour of God, that ye may be able to stand against the wiles of the devil. Ephesians 6:10,11

Certified, or convicted?

Will a certificate of vaccinated bring you real freedom?
In 250 AD, the Emperor Decius issued a decree demanding that everyone in the Roman Empire must perform a ritual sacrifice to the Roman gods.
These pagan sacrifices had to be witnessed by a Roman magistrate, who confirmed completion of the ritual with a certificate.
(Only Jews were exempt from this ritual.)

Many Christians were killed for refusing to betray their faith.
Many Christians went into hiding.

And many Christians betrayed their faith, followed the masses, and performed the pagan ritual to secure their 'freedom'.

When a person becomes a Christian, their heart changes.

Greater is he that is in you, than he that is in the world. 1 John 4:4

And when your heart changes, you see things differently: you have the inner ability to perceive what is truly right or wrong.
Often, a Christian cannot explain how or why something appears to be wrong, but your heart is screaming at you not to conform to whatever you are being tempted to accept and conform to.

Wide is the gate, and broad is the way that leadeth to destruction, and many there be that

go in thereat: Because straight is the gate, and narrow is the way, which leadeth unto life, and few there be that find it.   Matthew 7:13,14

And now it seems that our freedom may depend on whether or not we can produce a certificate of vaccination.

Christians were killed by decree of Emperor Decius because they refused to betray God in return for a certificate.

Personally, I believe it stinks that my freedom may be taken away because I refuse to accept a vaccine.

That we henceforth be no more children, tossed to and fro, and carried about with every wind of doctrine, by the sleight of men, and cunning craftiness, whereby they lie in wait to deceive.
Ephesians 4:14,15

I do not trust the multi-billionaires and shareholders of pharmaceutical companies who will further profit from a global vaccination and vaccine booster programme.

I do not trust the global corporations with their agenda to decide what the news is, what is included, and what is excluded.

I do not trust government statistics, because I know that statistics can be easily twisted to give whatever result the twister desires.

I do not trust the politicians who are making decisions on my behalf, (in fact, most politicians have yet to earn my respect, let alone my trust.)

Trust in the LORD with all thine heart; and lean not unto thine own understanding. In all thy ways acknowledge him, and he shall direct thy paths. Proverbs 3:5,6

Now is a time to stand up, step up, and speak up for Jesus.

This is not a time to be found neither hot nor cold.

A time is coming when everyone will be held accountable. And for many, it will be too late to do anything about it.

To the Christian of superficial faith, their eternal future is a terrifying thought; but to the person of real faith, it is one of the most comforting thoughts their heart can entertain.

The challenge to us now is to continue to grow in our trust in God's word, realising that in this chaotic world of deceptions and sinister agendas, despite the mess, God is in ultimate control, and all of these things and more must come to pass before the return of Jesus Christ.

Christians of conviction become comfortable.
Comfortable Christians become complacent.
Complacent Christians compromise.
Compromising Christians conform to the influences of the world.
And this, incrementally, is how Christians can quickly and easily fall away from Christ.

Don't lose your conviction.
Don't lose your confidence.
Don't lose your boldness.

Ye therefore, beloved, seeing ye know these things before, beware lest ye also, being led away with the error of the wicked, fall from your own stedfastness. 2 Peter 3:17

You are the head, and not the tail: you are above only, and not beneath. Deuteronomy 28:13

Do not bow your knee to anyone but Jesus: he is Lord of lords and King of kings.
Humble yourself only before Jesus.
Jesus is our only source of true hope.
Even when you are outnumbered, and mocked, and persecuted for standing up for your belief; when you are pressured by everyone around you to compromise your conviction to God, remember:
With God, you are always in the majority.

That at the name of Jesus every knee should bow, of things in heaven, and things in earth, and things under the earth: And that every tongue should confess that Jesus Christ is Lord, to the glory of God the Father.

Philippians 2:9-11

complacency compromise compliance conformity & Christ

Standing on the promises of Christ,
my King,
Through eternal ages let his praises ring;
Glory in the highest, I will shout and sing,
Standing on the promises of God.

Standing, standing,
Standing on the promises of God, my Saviour;
Standing, standing,
I'm standing on the promises of God.

Standing on the promises that cannot fail.
When the howling storms of doubt
and fear assail,
By the living Word of God I shall prevail,
Standing on the promises of God.

Standing on the promises of Christ, the Lord,
Bound to him eternally by love's strong cord,
Overcoming daily with the Spirit's sword,
Standing on the promises of God.

Standing on the promises I cannot fall,
Listening every moment to the Spirit's call,
Resting in my Saviour as my all in all,
Standing on the promises of God.

Standing on the Promises of Christ my King,
by Russell Kelso Carter, 1886

But if not

See then that ye
walk circumspectly,
not as fools,
but as wise,
redeeming the time,
because the days are evil.

Ephesians 5:15,16

Shame and fear

I bumped into a troubled friend recently; she was looking rather sheepish behind her mask, and rather fearful too.
It wasn't until later that I learnt that she was really concerned about her eternal future, (she has been especially troubled by the unceasing propaganda of fear that is proliferating just now).

Shame and fear: These two destructive emotions have been closely associated with each other for a very long time.
Let me take you way, way back to the beginning to explain.

In the garden of Eden, Adam and Eve enjoyed an abundance of blessings that we can only dream of. There they were living in bliss, in harmony with all of nature, and they enjoyed a close personal relationship with God: they needed for nothing.

(Because they didn't need anything, can you imagine what their conversations must have been like with God? communing with God was likely just continual praise of all that he is and all that he had created.)

But then it all went wrong: Eve was deceived into disobeying God; Adam quickly got involved too: and everything changed, especially in their relationship with God.

As a direct result of their disobedience, Adam and Eve did two very significant things:
They made clothes to cover themselves;
And they hid from God.

Why did they make clothes for themselves?
Because they were ashamed.

Why did they hide?
Because they were afraid.

Unless you have received forgiveness of your sins through Jesus Christ, you will also live in shame and fear.
If you want to replace your shame with confidence, and replace your fear for boldness – the only true way is through Jesus.

Adam and Eve became ashamed and fearful because of their sin.
But because Jesus has offered forgiveness of your sin, you do not need to be ashamed or fearful anymore.
Jesus undid what Adam and Eve caused by their disobedience.
And the person who deceived Eve: he has been defeated: he is a loser: he only has the power that you allow him to have over you, (and often his power is manifest in shame and fear).

Through Jesus, you need never live in shame or fear.
Through Jesus, the deceiver will lose his power over you.

So I ask: What are you ashamed of? and what are you afraid of? Do you like living ashamed and afraid? Or do you want to live a life that is confident and bold?

Your new life is freely available through everything that Jesus has already done for you. All you need to do is receive.

Now the serpent was more subtil than any beast of the field which the LORD God had made. And he said unto the woman, Yea, hath God said, Ye shall not eat of every tree of the garden?
And the woman said unto the serpent, We may eat of the fruit of the trees of the garden:
But of the fruit of the tree which is in the midst of the garden, God hath said, Ye shall not eat of it, neither shall ye touch it, lest ye die.
And the serpent said unto the woman, Ye shall not surely die:
For God doth know that in the day ye eat thereof, then your eyes shall be opened, and ye shall be as gods, knowing good and evil.
And when the woman saw that the tree was good for food, and that it was pleasant to the eyes, and a tree to be desired to make one wise, she took of the fruit thereof, and did eat, and gave also unto her husband with her; and he did eat.

And the eyes of them both were opened, and they knew that they were naked: and they sewed fig leaves together, and made themselves aprons.

And they heard the voice of the LORD God walking in the garden in the cool of the day: and Adam and his wife hid themselves from the presence of the LORD God amongst the trees of the garden.

And the LORD God called unto Adam, and said unto him, Where art thou?

And he said, I heard thy voice in the garden, and I was afraid, because I was naked: and I hid myself.

And he said, Who told thee that thou wast naked? Hast thou eaten of the tree, whereof I commanded thee that thou shouldest not eat?

And the man said, The woman whom thou gavest to be with me, she gave me of the tree, and I did eat.

And the LORD God said unto the woman, What is this that thou hast done? And the woman said, The serpent beguiled me, and I did eat.
Genesis 3:1-13

That was the cause of the problem.
This is the solution:

For God so loved the world, that he gave his only begotten Son, that whosoever believeth in him should not perish, but have everlasting life.
John 3:16

O soul, are you weary and troubled?
No light in the darkness you see?
There's light for a look at the Saviour,
And life more abundant and free!

Turn your eyes upon Jesus,
Look full in His wonderful face,
And the things of earth
will grow strangely dim,
In the light of His glory and grace

Through death into life everlasting,
He passed, and we follow Him there;
O'er us sin no more hath dominion
For more than conquerors we are!

His Word shall not fail you, He promised;
Believe Him, and all will be well:
Then go to a world that is dying,
His perfect salvation to tell!

Turn Your Eyes Upon Jesus,
by Helen Howarth Lemmel, 1922

He that walketh with
wise men shall be wise:
but a companion of fools shall
be destroyed.

Proverbs 13:20

Here am I; send me

"Forgive me for rudely interrupting," I rudely interrupted, "But did I just hear you say that you drove to Kazakhstan?"

"Er,...Yes!" The husband replied, "But actually we drove on, into Uzbekistan."

"You drove from Belfast to Uzbekistan!" I exclaimed.

"Aye, we did." And, smiling at his wife, he added, "And back again."

"Waow! You drove all the way from Belfast to Uzbekistan,... and back again." I repeated in astonishment.

"But isn't much of that just wilderness?"

"That's right," he replied, "in fact the only way of knowing that we were going in the right direction across the endless bumpy tundra was by following the trail of debris that previous vehicles had left behind: wheels, bumpers, doors, body panels, burnt out wrecks,..."

"Well, I guess you must have had a really resilient vehicle," I figured, "like a big four-by-four with reinforced suspension, and spare wheels, fuel cans, sand-tracks and shovels strapped to the outside?"

"No!" He hesitated, "Just a Suzuki Jimny."

"What????" I couldn't believe what I was hearing, "You drove from Belfast to Uzbekistan,... and back again,... in a Suzuki Jimny?"

"Yup!"

"But that's,..." I was flabbergasted, "...that's one of those little boxey cars that old ladies with pink hair drive about town at 20mph."

"Aye,... a Suzuki Jimny."

"But,... was it not wrecked by the time you got back to Belfast?"

"Nope! In fact when we got back we put it through the MOT, and it passed first time." He explained.

I was lost for words.

I apologised again for rudely interrupting, and thanked them for educating me.

Why is this modestly equipped adventure relevant?

From reading his word you will realise that God is not so much interested in your fitness, eloquence, wealth, knowledge, qualifications, or confidence.

These are all good qualities; but, God is not so interested in your abilities.

God is more interested in your availability.

Never feel unqualified when you are following Jesus; your only relevant qualification is your availability.

But God hath chosen the foolish things of the world to confound the wise; and God hath chosen the weak things of the world to confound the things which are mighty;

And base things of the world, and things which are despised, hath God chosen, yea, and things which are not, to bring to nought things that are: That no flesh should glory in his presence.
1 Corinthians 1:27-29

Consider some highly unqualified people that God has used powerfully:

Abraham and Sarah were too old!
Job was bankrupt!
Moses didn't like public speaking!
Joseph was abused!
Leah was plain!
Rahab was a prostitute!
David was an inexperienced boy!
And in his maturity, David was an adulterer and a murderer!
Gideon was timid!
Hosea had a broken marriage!
Jonah ran away!
Paul persecuted Christians!
Lazarus was dead!

So, what's your excuse?

But if not

Just as I am - without one plea,
But that Thy blood was shed for me,
And that Thou bidst me come to Thee,
O Lamb of God, I come!

Just as I am - and waiting not
To rid my soul of one dark blot,
To Thee, whose blood can cleanse each spot,
O Lamb of God, I come!

Just as I am - though toss'd about
With many a conflict, many a doubt,
Fightings and fears within, without,
O Lamb of God, I come!

Just as I am - poor, wretched, blind;
Sight, riches, healing of the mind,
Yea, all I need, in Thee to find,
O Lamb of God, I come!

Just as I am - Thou wilt receive,
Wilt welcome, pardon, cleanse, relieve;
Because Thy promise I believe,
O Lamb of God, I come!

Just as I am - Thy love unknown
Has broken every barrier down;
Now to be Thine, yea, Thine alone,
O Lamb of God, I come!

Just as I am - of that free love
The breadth, length, depth,
and height to prove
Here for a season, then above,
O Lamb of God, I come

Just As I Am, by Charlotte Elliot, 1835

But if not

Fear not therefore;
ye are of more value
than many sparrows.

Luke 9:6,7

End note

For Christians, living as exiles in this modern Babylon, where do we go from here?
Answer: we turn to the truth of God's word and the good news of Jesus Christ.

With devastating war in Eastern Europe, and ominous treats of a greater war spreading worldwide, it would be easy to fall into despair and fear.
But realise the truth that God is ultimately in control of everything.
Peace be with you.

Are not two sparrows sold for a farthing? and not one of them is forgotten before God?
But even the very hairs of your head are all numbered. Fear not therefore: ye are of more value than many sparrows.

[Luke 9:6,7]

The LORD bless thee
and keep thee:

The LORD make his face to
shine upon thee,
and be gracious unto thee:

The LORD lift up his
countenance upon thee,
and give thee peace.

Numbers 6:24-26

This book was written to encourage and inspire you; it was not intended to discourage or criticise you: I want you to realise all the many blessings that you can enjoy from God through Jesus Christ.

If I have discouraged you, or if you find reason to contradict the text of this book, please get in touch through the publisher so that your comments might be addressed in future revisions.

Love, light and peace,

Brian

Other books by the same author:

Alzheimer's Timeline
Prepare Yourself for China
The Broncle
成功企业的销售和营销秘笈
Raising a Smile
Bible Nuts & Bolts
Kircubbin (and hereabouts)

Printed in Great Britain
by Amazon